VINCE GILL

AN UNAUTHORIZED BIOGRAPHY
AND MUSICAL APPRECIATION
OF THE COUNTRY SUPERSTAR

VINCE GILL

AN UNAUTHORIZED BIOGRAPHY
AND MUSICAL APPRECIATION
OF THE COUNTRY SUPERSTAR

Mark Bego

RENAISSANCE BOOKS
Los Angeles

Library of Congress Catalog Card Number: 00-101884
ISBN: 1-58063-097-9

10 9 8 7 6 5 4 3 2 1

Design by James Tran

Published by Renaissance Books
Distributed by St. Martin's Press
Manufactured in the United States of America
First Edition

To Susan "Uzi" Mittelkauf

ACKNOWLEDGMENTS

The author would like to thank: Gene and Gloria Bego, Angela Bowie, Daphne Davis, Brad DeMeulenaere, Kara DeMeulenaere, A. J. Flick, Suzy Frank, Ron Goldfarb, Barbara and Bob Jonckers, Jack Kelly, Geri Lehman, Virginia Lohle (Star File Photos), Jim Parish, Shea Scullin, Barbara Shelley, Allan Taylor, Tom Tierney (BMG Archives, New York City), and Mary Wilson.

CONTENTS

INVINCIBLE

Until the 1990s, with the exception of Patsy Cline, I was never deeply into country music. To me, it all seemed to be about trite themes and twanging guitars. Being in New York City, and having lived through the 1970s disco era, my exposure to country songs was fleeting at best. Through my magazine work, I had met the lovely Dottie West when she headlined at the Lone Star Café in Manhattan, I had talked with Kenny Rogers at a cocktail party at the United Nations building, and I had interviewed Gary Morris when he performed the opera *La Bohème* with Linda Ronstadt at the Public Theater. All of this was my only real exposure to country music up to that time.

In 1990 I bought a house in Tucson, Arizona, and discovered a whole new world outside of Manhattan. Out of curiosity, on March 7, 1991, I bought tickets for the Judds in concert. I thought it would be fun to see what was happening in country music. I had no clue who the opening acts were on the evening's program, but I was curious. The support talent that night was Mark Chesnutt and Vince Gill. I couldn't believe the range and quality of music I heard that night. The next day, I bought a CD by each of the three acts.

Listening to Vince Gill's album *When I Call Your Name* (1989), I became an instant fan. As the decade progressed, I found increasingly, that the country music of the 1990s was closer to the kind of music that I preferred than the majority of the current pop music. In 1993 I was commissioned to write books on the contemporary men and women of country music. Those projects were my first forays into country, after a career of writing mainly about rock 'n' roll and rhythm and blues stars. The books I wrote that year became *Country Hunks* and *Country Gals*. In *Country Hunks*, one of the prominent stars was, of course, Vince Gill.

There just happens to be a golf course across the street from my neighborhood in Tucson, Arizona, called the Tucson National. One day in January of 1995, my friend Geri Lehman called and said, "You'll never guess who is going to be the celebrity golfer at the Northern Telecom golf tournament next week? Vince Gill!" Although I am not a huge golf fan, I knew that I didn't want to miss this event. My aunt and uncle were visiting at the time, and on the day that Vince was to golf, we packed our sunglasses and cameras and went to the links.

Predictably, Vince was quite a popular figure on the green that day. As we walked around and watched him play golf, I was amazed to see how approachable he was, how unaffected he was when fans came up to chat between holes and to ask for autographs. Finally, I decided to say hello. At the time I was writing the book *I Fall to Pieces: the Music and the Life of Patsy Cline,* so I thought it would be great to gain a quote from him about Patsy's musicianship. Not only was Gill polite and charming, but he also gladly gave me several wonderful quotes. "The greatest thing about Patsy Cline records is they still sound better than anything on the radio today, and this was thirty-five years ago!" he told me, and then elaborated. He was every bit as nice and friendly as everyone had said he was.

In June 1997 I again saw Vince in concert at the Tucson Convention Center, where he was headlining with Bryan White and special guest star LeAnn Rimes. He was amid the *High Lonesome Sound* tour, and it was an incredible evening of music. I was with two journalist friends, A. J. Flick and Susan Mittelkauf. All these two ladies could discuss was how sexy Vince looked on stage.

My most recent of many Vince sightings was in February 1999, when I attended the Grammy Awards with Mary Wilson of the legendary Supremes. At the Shrine Auditorium in Los Angeles we saw Gill sing the powerful ballad, "If You Ever Have Forever in Mind." A few minutes later we watched firsthand as Vince won his thirteenth Grammy Award, for that very same song.

Throughout the 1990s I have purchased all of Vince Gill's albums, and, as far as I am concerned, *High Lonesome Sound* (1996) is the ultimate—so far. (Of course all Vince Gill fans will have favorite albums of their own—and they are all discussed in detail in this book). Over the years, I have become quite an avid enthusiast of his music.

Having authored nearly forty books so far on show business and the music industry, it is always a special thrill to write about someone I admire—a person who is as charming and unpretentious as you would believe from watching him on television or hearing him speak on the radio. Preparing this book was fun, because it is about one of the most creative and coolest guys I have met in recent years, the multi-talented Vince Gill.

VINCE GILL

AN UNAUTHORIZED BIOGRAPHY
AND MUSICAL APPRECIATION
OF THE COUNTRY SUPERSTAR

ONE

KINDLY KEEP IT COUNTRY

He stands six feet three inches tall, has thick black hair, and presents a genuinely friendly smile. If his wardrobe choices are up to him, he prefers a casual Hawaiian shirt, jeans, and a pair of flip-flop sandals. He doesn't even own a cowboy hat. Although he is known for his phenomenal musical performances at the Ryman Auditorium in Nashville and the Grand Ole Opry, he is just as likely to be found in public teeing off at the nearest golf course. His music can be highly orchestrated pop, bluegrass, soul, Creole, or folk/rock. When he performs a duet, he is as at ease vocalizing with the likes of country songbirds Patty Loveless, Dolly Parton, and Reba McEntire, as he is with soul diva Gladys Knight, pop-singer Olivia Newton-John, or with blues rocker Bonnie Raitt. Although he seems like the most unlikely of country stars, that is exactly what he is. In fact, Vince Gill is the toast of today's Nashville.

His warm ballad singing, his emotionally insightful songwriting, and his easygoing "nice guy" image have made him one of the best known tenor voices in any genre of music. To merely label Vince Gill "a country star" does him an injustice, because his musical scope, his appeal, and his pure singing style encompass much more than just the sound of classic country. Through the years, his career has passed through several phases. In the late 1970s and early 1980s, Vince's first Top Ten hit was on the pop music charts as the lead singer of the group Pure Prairie League. You can still hear his rendition of the hit "Let Me Love You Tonight" on Top Forty radio. In the 1980s he had a disappointingly slow-burning solo career on RCA Records, which lasted for four albums: *Turn Me Loose* (1984), *The Things That Matter* (1985), *The Way Back Home* (1987), and *The Best of Vince Gill* (1989). In spite of flashes of brilliance and a handful of hits, he was still best known during that decade as "that singer/songwriter who is married to one of the members of Sweethearts of the Rodeo." It wasn't until 1989, when he signed with MCA Records and teamed with producer Tony Brown, that the creative fireworks began. Since then, it has been hit after hit and accolade after accolade for Gill.

When Nashville suddenly exploded in the early 1990s, it was a case of being in the right place at the right time for Vince. In February 1998, when he won his ninth Grammy Award for the song "Pretty Little Adriana," he staked his claim at the distinction of being the most highly decorated male singing star in country music. In the same decade he has won more than sixty-five separate industry awards, including Country Music Association Awards, TNN/*Music City News* Country Awards, *Music City News* Songwriter's Awards, Academy of Country Music Awards, BMI Awards, American Music Awards, and several more. Not only is he a hit in the United States, but he has also been named the Entertainer of the Year by the British Country Music Awards. Like his number-one hit single "Pocket Full of Gold" (1991), everything that Vince Gill touches seems to turn either to Gold or Platinum in album sales.

In the overall world of contemporary music, Vince Gill's appeal is amazingly wide. Not known simply as one of the biggest and most multi-talented country stars in the world, he has also garnered fans in the worlds of rock, folk, and contemporary Christian music, as well as gaining appreciators of his sensitive and appealing songwriting. Not wanting to be tied to only one genre, he has made a concerted effort to stretch stylistically. His late 1990s album, *High Lonesome Sound,* featured several New Orleans Cajun-style songs, more blues-oriented tunes, and more broad-based ballads, the latter of which lie somewhere in between country and pop/rock. In 1998, when his highly personal record, *The Key,* was released, it debuted at number one on the country album charts. It also marked a career turnabout, returning him to the 100 percent country-western sound that he had heard as a youngster on the radio and at home in Oklahoma. Always full of professional surprises—four months later—his second Christmas album, *Breath of Heaven,* found him crooning holiday tunes to a full orchestra, as though he were moving into Johnny Mathis territory.

In addition to his career achievements, Vince's personal life has also become big news lately, especially on the pages of the supermarket tabloids. It was in 1997 that he announced his eighteen-year marriage to Janis Gill, of the country music duo Sweethearts of the Rodeo, was over. Having just turned forty, was this part of a mid-life crisis, just another country union gone sour, or simply a major life overhaul? Since then, in the media he has been linked romantically with forty-year-old contemporary Christian singer Amy Grant, and with sexy twenty-eight-year-old country/rock singer Bekka Bramlett. Singing a duet with Olivia Newton-John at a music industry function in 1998, the gossip columnists nearly had him about to marry the *Grease* country/pop diva. Because he is steadfastly quiet about his personal life, Vince's fans still wonder which came first, a possible affair, or the divorce from Janis Gill?

Vince Gill's path to commercial success has been a gradual one. From a young age, in the early 1970s, he was torn between two loves: music and playing golf. Even today, he is one of the most famous and most sought-after golf-playing stars at celebrity tournaments in the United States. Career opportunities always seemed to fall into Vince's lap. For example, while still in high school he and a group of classmates formed a bluegrass band called Mountain Smoke. They gained so much local popularity that they were chosen as the opening act for country/rock group Pure Prairie League, when those musicians played in his hometown.

After graduating from high school, Vince was seriously considering becoming a professional golfer when he received a sudden offer to join Bluegrass Alliance, a bluegrass band based in Louisville, Kentucky. A year later, he moved to Los Angeles and joined another bluegrass band, Sundance, featuring famed fiddle player Byron Berline. Then, in 1978, when a guitar-playing spot in Pure Prairie League became available, Gill auditioned and ended up as the band's lead vocalist.

After three years and a trio of albums, Gill quit Pure Prairie League to join Rodney Crowell's band, the Cherry Bombs. The pianist in the Cherry Bombs was Tony Brown, who later became an executive at RCA Records in Nashville. Through his association with Tony Brown, Gill signed his first solo recording contract with RCA. During his six-year tenure with RCA, Vince recorded three pleasing albums of country/folk music. Releasing several singles off these albums, Gill scored his first Top Ten hit singles, including "Oklahoma Borderline" and "Cinderella." As he was preparing to leave the label, RCA released *The Best of Vince Gill*, which contained the debut of the first version of his song "I Never Knew Lonely."

When his RCA contract lapsed in 1989, Vince signed with MCA Records, and everything started to get exciting in his career. His debut album at MCA was produced by Tony Brown and was entitled *When I Call Your Name*. The title cut became a huge award-winning hit, and the album went on to sell more than a million copies. The avalanche of awards began almost immediately, when the song "When I Call Your Name" went on to win a Grammy Award and two Country Music Association Awards.

Gill's next albums, *Pocket Full of Gold* (1991) and *I Still Believe in You* (1992), respectively sold two and four million copies apiece, yielding a string of number-one successes including "Take Your Memory with You," "I Still Believe in You," "Don't Let Our Love Start Slippin' Away," "One More Last Chance," and "Trying to Get Over You." Vince's 1993 Christmas disc, "Let There Be Peace on Earth" also went platinum for a million copies sold. It was followed by his triple platinum album *When Love Finds You* (1994), which included the Top Ten smashes "Whenever You Come Around" and "What the Cowgirls Do." His 1995 greatest hits album, *Souvenirs,* was also certified platinum.

A highly sought-after star in the recording business, Vince has lent his talent to some of the most popular country-crossover albums of the 1990s. For example, on 1991's quadruple platinum album *Common Thread: The Songs of the Eagles,* he sang the classic rock ballad "I Can't Tell You Why." On the million-selling *Rhythm, Country and Blues* (1994), he teamed with soul star Gladys Knight to deliver the country-meets-Motown cut "Ain't Nothin' Like the Real Thing." And his duet with fellow Oklahoman Reba McEntire, "The Heart Won't Lie," went on to become a massive number-one selection when it was released with a dramatic video that showcased Gill's "country hunk" status to full advantage. Vince has also recorded songs for the soundtrack albums of feature films such as *Honeymoon in Las Vegas*

(1992), *Maverick* (1994), *8 Seconds* (1994), and *The Prince of Egypt* (1998).

Although most stars climb their way to the top of their profession by convincing people that they are bigger than life, Gill goes out of his way to project his true identity as a regular guy who happens to make music. He told the *Los Angeles Times* in September 1994: "I think sometimes people take their success and their career and their whole deal way too serious. I really don't. I'm still just a guitar player in my mind. I think that just comes from me being secure about myself. I wasn't any different ten years ago or twenty years ago. I just try to be normal. I like people. I'm approachable. It's not a conscious effort to be a certain way. I just am."

As superstars go, Vince Gill remains unchanged by fame. "I'll never get used to the recognition factor," he modestly stated in *TV Guide* magazine (October 1, 1994). "I went to a record store the other day and they happened to be playing my album. People stood there and stared at me, like they couldn't believe I would go shopping for CDs. A woman said, 'What are you doing here?' I told her I just wanted to buy some records. Then I did. I'm very approachable, very unassuming, and unlike some people, I try not to create a lot of hysteria."

Although other country stars wouldn't think of being seen in public without their trademark wigs, their sequins, their skin-tight jeans, or their trademark cowboy hats, Vince is too busy just being himself to care about fashion. As he told *Country Weekly* magazine in June 1998: "The bottom line for me is to find the cleanest shirt I have and go out there and just play. I played for so many years when I didn't have the luxury of a bag full of hit records to perform. Now I have some hits, I still don't plan my shows around some big visual type setting. I want people to come and hear us play and sing—not to see a bunch of bottle rockets go off. I do what I do and what I have always done."

His philosophy for living a life that fame has touched goes back to the very beginning. His late father, Stan Gill, who was a lawyer and later a judge, once told him, "It's all for nothin' if you don't stay the same." Taking that advice to heart, Vince remains the same unaffected singer and guitar player he was when he started out in this business as a teenager. His unassuming and approachable personality has remained one of the prime keys to his incredible career success.

Instead of being overly serious about his singing career, Gill laughingly insisted to *Country Weekly* in March 1998: "Music is my hobby, golf is my life." But his fans already knew that. After Vince won the prestigious Entertainer of the Year Award from the Country Music Association in 1993, he startled music fans when he announced in *TV Guide* in 1994: "A reporter asked me which was more exciting: getting a hole in one or winning Entertainer of the Year. I said that the hole in one was more exciting—it's something that I had waited my whole life for—and that winning Entertainer of the Year was more surprising."

Gill has proven repeatedly that he is the most unlikely country star in the business today and is virtually unfazed by his critics. On the subject of his totally un-country singing style, critic Richard Cromelin proclaimed in the *Los Angeles Times* (September 24, 1994): " 'Look at Us' and 'I Still Believe in You' [are] classic records that are closer to Smokey Robinson than *Smokey and the Bandit.*" Vince admittedly didn't set out to become a country singer; his goal was simply to make good music that he genuinely enjoyed. If millions of people liked it: great!

Oddly enough, not all of Vince's heartfelt signature songs are about life, love, and happiness. Each of his last three non-holiday albums have featured sad numbers about death and loss. "Go Rest High on That Mountain," "Pretty Little Adriana," and "The Key to Life" are each about the untimely passing of people who have deeply touched Gill's life. He is unafraid to tackle these topics head-on. "A lot of positive things can come out of emotions that are sad. I don't agree with the perception that sad songs always have to be depressing. I love to hear songs that are blue. Things go on, and you don't need . . . [to sing] about how 'beautiful' life is," he detailed to *TV Guide* for its issue of September 15, 1993.

When his 1998 album, *The Key,* debuted on the charts at number one, it gave Vince a thrilling new high-water mark on which to gauge his professional fame. One of the most in-demand, most popular performers in today's country music, his fascinating life story also intersects the lives and careers of some of the biggest stars in the music world. They include such luminaries as Dolly Parton, Reba McEntire, LeAnn Rimes, George Jones, Patty Loveless, Bonnie Raitt, Mark Knopfler of Dire Straits, Alison Krauss, Sweethearts of the Rodeo, Michael McDonald, Gladys Knight, and Emmylou Harris.

What is the key to Vince Gill's incredibly broad-based appeal? How does it feel to be one of the leading stars to bring country music into the forefront in the 1990s? What brought about the sudden breakup of his long-term marriage? How does Gill juggle his golf tournaments, awards shows, and charity events with his demanding music career? What is the reality about the rumors of his speculated-about affairs with the high-profile women now in his life? Where do his professional convictions lie? Is he always the ultimate "nice guy" the press portrays him to be? The answers to these questions define the fascinating public and private life of country music's most popular balladeer. The man in question— with a pocket full of gold and a voice full of conviction—is unquestionably country music's most unlikely superstar. This is Vince Gill.

TWO

THAT OKLAHOMA SWING

By country music standards, Vince Gill's childhood was so untypically Nashville it was downright suburban. He did *not* grow up in the rodeo circuit, he was *not* raised on a farm, and he did not wear cowboy duds. His father was not a rancher nor a honky-tonk singer nor a coal miner. The closest Vince ever came to milking a cow, roping a steer, or being in close proximity with other ranch animals occurred when he hit a "birdie" on the local golf course.

Born on April 12, 1957, in Norman, Oklahoma, Vincent Grant Gill was the middle child in a family of three children. His mother, Jerene, was a homemaker and a hairdresser. His father, Stan, was a lawyer who later became an appellate court judge (Mr. Gill also played the piano, the guitar, and the banjo.) In addition, the Gill household included an older brother, Bobby, and a younger sister, Gina.

Located about twenty miles south of downtown Oklahoma City, Norman in the late 1950s was a typical American suburb of the (President Dwight) Eisenhower era. The year that Vince was born, Ford Motor Company debuted the Edsel car, *I Love Lucy* was the number-one series on television, and Elvis Presley scored four number-one hit singles—dominating the top spot in

Billboard magazine's Top 100 chart twenty-six weeks out of that year.

When Vince was asked by *Modern Screen's Country* magazine (Fall 1991) to describe his childhood, he responded, "Normal. I lived across the street from a grade school. I played high school baseball and basketball. . . . I'm real proud of the upbringing I had."

When Vince was five years old, his family moved to nearby Oklahoma City. Vince's cousin, Robert Simpson, now a farmer in Piedmont, Oklahoma, recalled in the *National Enquirer* (December 25, 1993) that, at the time, Vince and his older brother, Bobby, were nearly inseparable. "Wherever Bobby went, he took his baby brother with him," said Simpson. "Bobby would push him on the swings and Bobby taught Vince how to ride a bike."

In Nashville terms, Ralph Emory is to country music as Dick Clark is to rock 'n' roll. In his position as a disc jockey, and the host of *The Ralph Emory Show* and TNN's *Nashville Now*, he has interviewed the biggest country celebrities for decades. In his book *The View from Nashville* (1998), he recounts an amusing story about young Gill. According to Emory, "Vince's mother, Jerene Gill, once showed me what her son gave her for Christmas back when he was seven years old. It was a bottle of Tarn-X Silver Polish. Vince laughs about it today, suggesting he was even then hoping to line her walls with platinum albums, and he'd seen her clean her silver with toothpaste once too often."

It isn't any wonder that music became an interest of his as a child. Vince remembers the house being filled with music when he was growing up. His banjo-playing father would teach his offspring songs from his own childhood. Both Mr. and Mrs. Gill sang around the house, inspiring their children to do the same.

It wasn't long before Vince was able to differentiate notes and mimic the sounds he heard on the guitar. Both of his parents had a musical background and an appreciation of all sorts of musical styles. Hence, they were very supportive of his musical aspirations. Vince has been blessed with the ability to hear music in a way that allows him to sing and play instinctively "by ear."

Looking back on his childhood musical influences, Vince remembers that they ranged from classic country and western music to rock 'n' roll. "It's a pretty diverse list," he told Robyn Flans of *Country Fever* magazine (May/June 1994), "beginning with Jim Reeves and Patsy Cline, Buck Owens, Merle Haggard. Then I got a little older, and it became the Beatles, Led Zeppelin, and people like Canned Heat. My brother was a big blues fan, and he played me some really neat records as a kid. I played one of my first gigs with my brother at about eight or nine [years old] at a radio station."

Even now, Vince still recalls vividly when he realized that he had found his singing voice. He remembers riding in the family automobile with his parents and noticing a little vibrato in his voice. When it came out, even he was startled to hear it. (He would turn that trademark vibrato into his signature singing style, which is now legendary.)

One of the Gills' neighbors was later to recount that even when Vince was very young, he was very musical. She recalls going over to the Gill house for Jerene Gill to style her hair. While there she would see shy little Vince pounding on one toy or another, keeping time, as if he were accompanying some sort of music in his head.

When Vince was eight years old, a tragedy occurred in the family, which left a deep emotional scar. His older brother, Bobby, was involved in a car accident. Although he survived the wreck, he sustained a head injury from which he was never to recover. From that point on, Bobby was never able to maintain a normal train of thought.

Vince explained later to *Country Weekly* magazine (August 7, 1999): "He had a car wreck when he was twenty-two. He had been drinking and he hit a semi going 100 miles an hour. He was in a coma for several months and they didn't give him a chance to live."

Bobby's car accident had a profound effect on Vince. He saw first-hand how short and precious life could be. After the accident, everything seemed to change in Vince's young life. It broke his heart to see his normally happy and energetic brother reduced to a young man who couldn't sustain a flow of thought for more than a few minutes at a time. As Vince grew up, their roles reversed, with Vince taking care of older brother Bobby, in much the same way Bobby used to look after his little sibling.

Bobby was to spend the duration of his life unable to drive a car, hold a job, or ever have any sense of independence. Witnessing what happened to his brother as a result of the accident, Vince was determined to jump headlong toward the goals he wanted to accomplish. He feared that some horrifying twist of fate could rob him of the potential he knew he had within.

In a *National Enquirer* article of December 28, 1993, an unidentified Gill family member was quoted as saying, "[Vince] told me, 'Life is so unfair. Why was Bobby's future stolen from him? Whatever I do, I'm going to be the best. I'm going to do it for Bobby.'"

For a while, Vince set his sights on becoming a major league baseball player. In the same *National Enquirer* piece, a family friend observed, "No matter what Vince did, it was always important for him to be the best, the winner. He really hated to lose." Whenever the ball team did lose a game, Gill took it personally, wanting to make every moment of his life count. "His dad would walk off with Vince crying on his shoulder," that same source recalled.

Vince began to take everything in life quite seriously. He grew up with a strong sense of right and wrong, and if he was unjustly criticized, he would verbally lash out in defense.

One of his classmates from Grover Cleveland Elementary School remembered for the *National Enquirer* in late 1993: "Once when we were in the sixth grade, a teacher was being really critical of how Vince did his homework. Vince furiously told off this teacher. Then he stormed out of the classroom, slamming the door behind him. We were all shocked and also full of awe. In those days, you just didn't talk back to a teacher or get angry with one."

When he was asked about his favorite Christmas while growing up, Vince points to December 25, 1967. By then, the music of the psychedelic-era Beatles had swept America—the year that their *Sgt. Pepper's Lonely Hearts Club Band and Magical Mystery Tour* album topped the charts. "I was ten years old," Vince has recalled with enthusiasm in *Country Fever* magazine (February 1993), "and I got a Gibson [ES-335] electric guitar for Christmas and a Fender super reverb amp. I'll never forget that. They had it hidden in the closet. It was really neat, because I kinda started to get it that Mom and Dad really thought I had some talent. I still play that guitar and still use that amp, twenty-six years later. And it showed me that they had a lot of support in me: 'We approve of what you're doing; here's some great tools to learn with.' It was neat."

That Christmas present forever changed Vince's life. Mastering the guitar became his primary goal and obsession. On his own he sought out record albums that featured proficient guitar playing so he could learn to emulate the sound. Which albums did he recall learning the most from? "Any and all Chet Atkins records, especially *Chet Atkins Picks on the Beatles.* I couldn't believe how he played," Vince explained in *Country Guitar* magazine (Summer 1995).

Vince's other main interest as a kid was sports. His favorite activities included hockey, football, and golf. So far as having a preferred spectator sport, he said in *Country Weekly* magazine (March 3, 1998): "I love the game of hockey. We had a really good Boston Bruins farm team in Oklahoma City where I grew up. I saw a lot of good hockey players and actually have some knowledge of the game and [I] enjoy it."

Gill told *Country Music* magazine, for its March/April 1997 issue, that his father, Stan, was quite the disciplinarian. "My dad was pretty strict, and there was a fear factor that worked. And, I'm glad! I mean, at the time I was probably thinkin' it would wear me out. But I was afraid to go get drunk and get thrown in jail. He'd kick my butt! And now, I'm really thankful. Some of that fear was a good fear."

Earlier, Vince told *Modern Screen's Country* (May 1992): "If I screwed up, he busted my butt. Both of my parents ruled pretty heavy-handed, and properly so. They made you treat people right. They didn't let you act like a fool. If you got in trouble, you were in trouble!"

As a teenager, attending Northwest Classen High School in Oklahoma City, Vince was quite a serious student who, seemingly, couldn't be coerced into mischief. He never found himself bowing to adolescent peer pressure as a youth. He was never led into drinking beer or smoking cigarettes in an attempt at being "cool." Even by Oklahoma standards of the day, he found that his passion for country and bluegrass music was considered very odd, and very square. While others his age were into the music of Ted Nugent, KISS, and Alice Cooper, teenager Gill was dabbling into the music of Bill Monroe and Flatt & Scruggs. Anyone his age listening to such hillbilly-like country stuff in the early 1970s was sure to be labeled a total geek. Obviously, Vince could not have cared less.

Being basically a self-taught guitar player, Vince slowly figured out how to make different styles of sounds come out of his instrument. "I remember trying to learn how to play rock 'n' roll," he recalled in *Best of Country Guitar Player* magazine in 1993. "I couldn't figure out how guys bent the strings to get vibrato, because I didn't know anything about slinky strings. I went to a music store when I was about twelve or thirteen [years old] and asked how those guys got the note to hang on like that. The sales-man said, 'Oh, you've got to buy one of *these*,' and sold me a Vox treble-bass booster. All it did was make a racket."

Discussing his famous son's turning point in his musical aspi-rations, Stan Gill recalled in the Fall 1994 issue of *People Country* magazine: "I didn't doubt his talent, but frankly I didn't expect him to gain the success he has. He got to be about thirteen and figured out how much girls liked it."

While in his teens, Vince began stretching musically. He was interested in a wide range of genres, from country, to rock, to folk/rock. Looking back on this period in his life, it is easier to understand why Gill's music today has such diversity. Describing what he personally liked to listen to as a kid in *Modern Screen's Country Music* magazine (Fall 1991), Vince said, "Everything from Buck Owens to Canned Heat. Patsy Cline. Jim Reeves. My sister kept playing Crosby, Stills & Nash records, and she got me into James Taylor. I dug rock 'n' roll too, like Led Zeppelin, the Doobie Brothers, the Allman Brothers, any brothers I guess!"

Vince was fondly thought of as a nice and helpful teenage boy in the neighborhood. Nancy Tiernan recalled for the *National Enquirer* (December 28, 1993): "I remember when Vince was just fifteen and my children were younger, that he would play with them and pick them up and take care of them. I thought it really unusual in a boy that young, but Vince was always a super nice kid."

According to country music commentator/host Ralph Emory in his *The View from Nashville* (1998), Vince always had a sharp sense of humor and a quick wit: "He was always fast on the draw. When he signed up for a junior football league the coach tossed him a ball and asked him if he thought he could pass it. 'Pass it? I don't think I can even swallow it,' Vince quipped."

Gill continued to have an interest in all sorts of sports throughout his school years. At one point while he was a teenager, he daydreamed of one day having a career as an athlete. His first consideration was not football or golf; it was baseball. However, he was still too young to have defined his path in life.

By the 1970s, high-schooler Vince dismissed his dreams of being a major league baseball player. He had lost interest enough to completely pass on even trying out for his school's varsity team. It was at this time that he threw himself headlong into the game of golf. At Northwest Classen High School, Vince was ranked as the number-two player, and his friend, Phillip Slinkerd, was ranked at number one.

According to Slinkerd in the *National Enquirer* (December 29, 1993): "Those of us on the high school golf team always knew he would make it big one day. When we would go off on golf trips to play in tournaments away from home, Vince brought his guitar. He would say, 'Give me a topic,' and on the spot he would make up a song, complete with incredibly good lyrics that matched and rhymed perfectly. We were astounded at his ability to do this so well."

Explaining his career decision to be a musician, Vince later told writer Deborah Barnes of *New Country* magazine for its issue of June 1997, "They often say, 'He could've been a pro golfer instead of a musician.' I didn't make that statement. [Press interviewers] would just say, 'What would you have tried to do if you weren't a musician?' And I'd say, 'Well, I would've tried to play golf.' So then it's [imitating an announcer]: 'He gave up a career as a professional golfer . . .' It gets kind of blown up and all that. It's fine to dream, you know, but I function a lot better in a very realistic approach to things. And the reality of it is I'm probably not [a] good enough [golfer]."

To have extra spending money in his pocket, teenage Vince had several after school jobs. At one point he worked at a local pizza parlor. Looking back on it for *Country Weekly* magazine (August 17, 1999), Vince says, "My first job was making pizzas at the Pizza Inn. That was a blast because pizza was my favorite food in the world—and still is. So, I'd make mistakes on purpose just so I could take them home and give them to my family. We used to do some mean things. I spiked a kid's pizza one time with jalapenos, red pepper, and all kinds of hot things. He had to drink about eight Cokes with his pizza. He came up to pay for it and said, 'Man, your sausage is so *hot!*' "

Not surprisingly, one of Gill's other jobs was working at a local golf course. He was also planning on continuing his education after high school graduation by attending college.

He was a golfer all through his last six years in school, and at the time he considered it as a possible profession. Pondering his options after high school, he figured that he could either try to play on the Professional Golf Association (PGA) circuit, attend college and play golf on a college team, or he could blow off golf and become a professional musician. All three choices held a certain appeal for him.

At that point, Vince chose to focus his energy on music. When he did so it was one of those "it's now or never" decisions. His determination and enthusiasm were so strong that he abandoned his plans to attend college.

It was while still in high school that Vince had put together his first band. They called themselves Mountain Smoke. The six-member outfit consisted of a yard-sprinkler-system installer, two bankers, a college student, and high-schooler Vince, who played guitar in the group and sang.

Gill will never forget the group's first professional gig. What should have been a triumphant experience turned out to be a painful memory, when the local woman who hired them to play at one of her social events refused to pay them. "We got stiffed," Vince recounted in *Country Fever* magazine (May/June 1994). "My dad was a lawyer and said, 'Take her to court,' so we did, and I acted as the lawyer. The judge said, 'You're suing this lady for $100 for services rendered. Are you aware she's countersuing you for slander and libel and . . . blah, blah, blah?' A real lawyer stood up, opened his briefcase, looked at me, and said, 'Do you want to pursue this?'" With that, Vince and his buddies chose to cut their losses and walk away.

Things did improve for Vince and his Mountain Smoke buddies. The band developed into a popular success. They were making money playing local gigs and supporting themselves. What more could they want? They were even booked as the opening act when the noted band Pure Prairie League came to Oklahoma City for a local concert. Gill was only sixteen at the time, but already he was receiving an inside glimpse of the professional side of the legitimate music business.

Without a doubt, the strangest experience that happened to Mountain Smoke, as a band, was one that found them booked to open for the heavy-duty rock group KISS in Oklahoma City. Vince explained how that happened in *TV Guide* (October 1, 1994): "That had to have come out of somebody's bad imagination. The opening act canceled at the last minute, and they called us to play. It was bizarre."

The word bizarre hardly even does the situation justice. At the time, KISS had recorded their first three albums: *KISS* (1974), *Hotter Than Hell* (1974), and *Dressed to Kill* (1995). Comprised of Gene Simmons, Paul Stanley, Peter Criss, and Ace Frehley, this quartet is known as much for their Kabuki from Mars makeup and space age outfits as they are for their hard-rocking music. Their concert shows to this day are still known for their outrageous staging, massive light shows, and fiery pyrotechnics. Imagine this little bluegrass band trying open a show like that!

Vince has recalled that it was around 6:00 P.M. when he and the band received a call from a local promoter, asking them if they could assemble themselves and arrive at the local Civic Center by eight that night. Thinking it was just another gig, Gill and the group hurried to make it on time. When they arrived at the venue, the marquee out front was emblazoned with the word: *KISS*. Vince was convinced that KISS must be performing the following night and that they were being hired to play a Shriners' Convention or some other staid event that required a bluegrass band.

Much to their surprise, it was really KISS they were opening for that evening! Picture the looks on the audience's faces when Mountain Smoke stepped out on that stage with their fiddles and banjos, probably about the time the concertgoer's first joint had kicked in. Talk about "wrong audience/wrong band." The idea of seeing a bluegrass group open for KISS is perhaps the craziest thing on record, second only to Jimi Hendrix opening for the Monkees in the late 1960s. Needless to say, the crowd that night started booing and hissing the minute Mountain Smoke began to play. Vince and the band lasted only four or five songs into their set. To this day, Gill regards this as the most hostile crowd in all of his career.

As Mountain Smoke hastily left the stage at the end of their truncated set, Vince loosened his jeans, dropped them, and mooned the booing crowd. To further punctuate his distraught feelings, Gill flipped them "the bird" and stormed off stage.

The reviewer from the *Tulsa* (Oklahoma) *World* newspaper recalls seeing the "full moon" à la Gill that night, proclaiming in his review of the show, "Vince Gill showed what part of his anatomy the crowd could kiss."

Although at the time it was a traumatic booking from hell, Vince now can look back on that scene with humor. Later (October

1, 1994) he recounted in *TV Guide:* "People were screaming, booing. Anything that could be hurled—shoes, bottles, cans—came at the stage. A couple of guys in the band were mad, but I found the absurdity of the situation to be hysterical. We were like that band in [the 1984 movie *This Is*] *Spinal Tap.*"

Mountain Smoke's union seemed to encompass one insane gig after another. Describing another fiasco, Vince told *Upbeat* magazine in January 1998: "There was this one time that I will not forget as long as I live. We were playing at a college. They made a mistake and booked us during spring break. We got about twelve people. It's amazing but it's not the shows at the big arenas that you remember so much as the strange ones in the twenty plus years I've been doing this."

Vince always looks back with fondness on those days with his first band. "A lot of firsts in that band. But that's a little personal," he acknowledged in *Country Fever* magazine in mid-1994. "That's where I really got to do a lot of traveling and see a lot of the country. We toured in a motor home, and I made a lot of connections through the bluegrass music that eventually even got me into rock 'n' roll."

Mountain Smoke's combination of rock 'n' roll and bluegrass became quite successful in the Oklahoma City area, and Vince became hooked on the music scene. For Gill, one opportunity just seemed to lead into the next. His transitions from band to band over the next few years support the fact that natural career paths seemed to open up to him, one after another. For example, right after graduating from high school in 1975, a friend called and insisted that Gill join the bluegrass band, the Bluegrass Alliance. Vince said yes to the offer, then packed his van and left to join the well-known group in Kentucky.

It was Gill's growing proficiency as a guitar player—particularly as a bluegrass guitar picker—that first made people gravitate toward him. According to Vince, as he told *Country Fever:* "People wanted me to play in their bluegrass bands because I could sing. And that was odd in itself, because up to then people wanted to work with me because I could play. But then I started soaking up acoustic music and [using a] flatpicking [playing style] on the acoustic guitar. That led me to want to play the mandolin, dobro, and banjo." It wasn't long before Vince discovered that audiences liked to hear his expressive tenor voice as much as they enjoyed his guitar playing in Mountain Smoke.

Moving to Louisville, Kentucky, to be a part of the Bluegrass Alliance group brought further new opportunities to Gill. As he explained to *Country Fever* magazine in the mid-1980s: "In a sense, it was because there were a lot of great players who lived up in that area. That's where Ricky Skaggs came out of, and I played in a band called Boone Creek with him for a while. [The band members] didn't hit it off real well, so I didn't last too long. Too many chiefs and not enough Indians."

To polish his style, Vince would seek out records that had great guitar playing on them, gleaning different things from an assortment of well-known guitarists. He told *Country Guitar* for its summer 1995 issue: "For that lightning stuff—James Burton and Albert Lee. I'd always hear James and not realize it, 'cause he was on all those Elvis records. But the one record that turned it around for me was *Luxury Liner* [1977] by Emmylou Harris, which featured Albert [Lee]. . . . When I heard [him], his sound really spoke to me. I knew I could adapt those type of lines with all the open strings and rolls and everything, to my bluegrass style."

With regard to singing in the band Boone Creek, Vince recalled in the *Gavin Report* (March 8, 1991): "Nobody knew I was in the band because I never did any recording with them. Actually I got fired from that band, and it was the best job I ever lost. I moved to California right after that, and that's where I ran into Rodney [Crowell] and Emmy[lou Harris] and Albert [Lee], my cronies who I really like."

Moving from band to band while he was still an impression-able teenager, Gill was able to learn many styles of music and become proficient at all of them. From Mountain Smoke to Blue-grass Alliance to Boone Creek, he was able to build up his self-confidence, his guitar playing, and his singing skills. Now it was time for him to try more challenging career moves. At that time there was more country-tinged country music coming out of Cali-fornia than there was anywhere in disco-obsessed New York City, so it seemed a natural choice for him to move to the West Coast. At the age of nineteen, Vince Gill sought his fortune in the land of golden musical opportunity.

THREE

LET ME LOVE YOU TONIGHT

Vince realized that the musical competition would be as great on the West Coast as it was on the East Coast, but there was already a California rock sound that had proven very successful for such talents as Linda Ronstadt, the Nitty Gritty Dirt Band, the Eagles, the Byrds, and Jackson Browne. It was a style of music that often blended folk/rock music with country and western sounds. The fusion of this style is best personified by two of the most successful and influential albums of the era: Ronstadt's *Heart Like a Wheel* (1975) and the Eagles' *Hotel California* (1976).

When Gill first arrived in the Los Angeles area as a teenager, the initial band with which he performed was Bryon Berline & Sundance. It was 1976, and Vince was nineteen years old. He began playing guitar with Bryon's group. When banjo player John Hickman quit, Vince was asked to play the banjo as well. Although it was not his first choice of musical instruments, he proved to be quite a proficient banjo player.

On one hand, it sounds very fickle to hop from one band to another the way Vince did. None of these bands, however, were paying him a significant amount of money. Gill felt that it was in his own best interest to gain as much experience as possible with each group, and then move on to a new musical opportunity.

Singer/songwriter Rodney Crowell recalls his initial introduction to Gill and his music. The first time they met was in 1976 at the Los Angeles rock 'n' roll nightclub the Troubadour. Gill was on stage with Bryon Berline's band, and all of a sudden he started singing one of Crowell's compositions, "'Til I Gain Control Again." Rodney was stunned and flattered. They were destined to become lifelong friends.

Looking back on this early era of his show business career, Vince remembers it fondly. As he said to *Country Music* (March/April 1997), "My favorite days are still back when I was playin' bluegrass and we'd split the money up behind the stage when we got off."

As Gill hopped in and out of bands, there was no clear-cut career path that he was following. He proceeded purely on instinct. Instead of plotting things out, he has always found that one professional door led to another professional door, and there were opportunities behind all of them. Here he was, only nineteen, and he was playing on stage in Los Angeles opening for several of his biggest idols: Emmylou Harris, Rodney Crowell, and Dolly Parton.

Vince was also becoming quite proficient at playing a number of different instruments as well. Among others, he has mentioned the electric guitar—steel and bass, the mandolin, and the banjo. He was a true utility man, which put him much in demand.

In addition to the California folk/rock sound of the era, several musicians on the West Coast were blending rock, pop, folk, bluegrass, rhythm and blues, and jazz together. One of the most visible performers at the time was Linda Ronstadt. Her album *Hasten Down the Wind* (1976) mixed reggae ("Rivers of Babylon"), country ("Crazy"), and classic rock ("That'll Be the Day"). She bridged the gap between rock and country, impressively scoring Top Ten hits on both charts in 1977.

The Doobie Brothers, who were one of Vince's favorite groups, also shifted from hard rock to jazz-infused rock in the mid-1970s, when Michael McDonald joined the group. McDonald's first two albums with the group, *Takin' It to the Streets* (1976) and *Livin' on the Fault Line* (1977), immediately expanded their already appealing sound. Unsurprisingly, he left another jazz fusion/rock band, Steely Dan, to become a Doobie Brother.

Especially experimental with blending jazz with rock and folk at the time was Joni Mitchell, whose albums *Court and Spark* (1974), *The Hissing of Summer Lawns* (1975), and *Heijra* (1976) not only embraced jazz, they oozed it. These three releases helped Mitchell expand beyond being thought of as only a folk/rock legend. On all three of these albums, she was not only supported musically by rockers such as David Crosby, Neil Young, James Taylor, and Graham Nash, but she blended their sound with such jazz stars as Tom Scott, Jaco Pastorius, Joe Sample, and Larry Carlton.

One of the most influential musicians Vince Gill was exposed to at the time was guitarist Larry Carlton. A native of Torrance, California, Carlton first came to fame as part of the jazz/fusion group the Crusaders. His work on Joni Mitchell's aforementioned trio of albums and other notable session work led to his own solo recording career, which began in 1978. His guitar solo on the song "Third World Man" from Steely Dan's album *Gaucho* (1980) can be heard as a staple on both jazz and rock radio stations to this day. He won Grammys in 1981 for the song "Theme from *Hill Street Blues*" by Mike Post featuring Larry Carlton, in the category of Best Pop Instrumental Performance, and in the same category in 1987 for his recording of the Doobie Brothers' "Minute By Minute." (In 1988 an intruder broke into Carlton's recording studio and shot Larry in the neck. After several months of physiotherapy, he was able to make a full recovery and continue his musical career. He currently records for jazz label GRP Records.)

One night in California, Vince was playing with the band Sundance at a nightclub in Redondo Beach, a small coastal community located about an hour's drive south of Hollywood. Known for its laid-back lines of surfing shops, taverns, restaurants, and bars, this small beach community was the perfect proving ground for up-and-coming bands. At the club where Sundance was booked, the opening act that night was a female country/folk duo who called themselves Sweethearts of the Rodeo. The group consisted of two singing sisters, Janis and Kristine Oliver. They were born in nearby Torrance, California, and raised in Manhattan Beach. They were the daughters of a phone company worker dad and a homemaker mom. Fascinated with the country/rock fusion sound coming out of the Los Angeles area, they started singing as a harmonizing acoustic duet in 1973. The two of them sang, and Janis also accompanied them on guitar. They had taken their act's name from a Byrds album: *Sweethearts of the Rodeo* (1968).

That night in Redondo Beach, Vince and Janis had a chance meeting on the stairs that led up to the small stage. She was just leaving the performing area as he was heading to the stage. Gill never forgot that special moment.

Janis was a petite brunette with a winning smile and sparkling brown eyes. She left an indelible impression on him and obviously touched his heart. It was a case of love at first sight. He was impressed with her unique Slavic features and her almond-shaped eyes.

At the time, Janis was twenty-two years old, and Vince was only nineteen. Janis has recalled for Mike Kosser in *Hot Country* (1993): "It just wasn't right then. [Later,] when the guy I was seeing and the girl he [Vince] was seeing dumped us at the same time, we decided it might be a good time to give it a whirl. It didn't take two weeks for [me] to see that it was serious."

Like Vince, Janis and her sister were into the sounds of classic country music as well. According to Janis, while their high

44

school friends were listening to rock 'n' roll, she and Kristine were bewitched by the sound of Nashville. While their contemporaries were rocking out to the *Rolling Stones,* or getting caught up in the whole disco craze, they went off into an entirely different musical direction. As Janis told *People* magazine (June 10, 1991): "We were hooked on country. Anything to stand out."

Vince was later to recall that Janis was very reticent to get involved with him. He was, however, convinced that they were destined to be together, even if she was then much more sophisticated than he. Instead of going out with one another as a couple, they ended up becoming really good friends who liked to hang out together. Yet, in the back of his mind, Gill was always serious about their relationship. This particular phase of their union went on during 1977, 1978, and 1979. Finally, their feelings blossomed into a romance, and they moved in together.

While all of this was going on, an opportunity came along that changed Vince's life and his career. He learned that Pure Prairie League was looking for a new singer/guitar player to front for them because Craig Lee Fuller was leaving the group. It was Fuller who wrote and sang the song "Amie." Although the song was recorded in the early 1970s, it didn't become a hit until 1975. It wasn't long afterward that Fuller left the band. This proved to be the perfect window of opportunity for Gill.

According to Vince, the band had already gone through dozens of players in their quest to find someone who could not only sing, but write music and play the guitar impressively. When the remaining members of Pure Prairie League approached Gill and asked him to join them, they told him what they were looking for and outlined the position in which they presently found themselves. They had gigs booked and a record deal with a major label. It all sounded very appealing to Vince. He took a few days to consider the offer. Then he suggested to the band that they play together to see what kind of chemistry existed among them. When they did, everything clicked, and, suddenly, Vince found himself playing rock 'n' roll for the next five years of his life.

Not only did Gill land a gig with a hot band, but he also found himself with his first record deal, one that was going to launch his songwriting career as well. For Vince, this was just another instance of having the good instinct and the good fortune to be at the right place at the right time. Although he was younger than the rest of Pure Prairie League, he fit right in. He had the exact sound they needed, both as a singer and as a guitar player.

When the band asked Gill to join them, they also inquired if he had any songs that they might consider recording. He had half a dozen songs he played for them, and they loved them all. According to Vince in *Country Weekly* magazine (June 22, 1999), songwriting was a whole new ballgame for him: "I didn't try to write songs until I was nineteen or maybe twenty years old. You have to work on it and practice. There are a lot of lame songs nobody is ever going to hear."

Pure Prairie League was originally formed in Cincinnati, Ohio, in 1971. At the time the band included Craig Lee Fuller on vocals and guitar, George Powell on vocals and guitar, John Call on pedal steel guitar, Jim Lanham on bass, and Jim Caughlin on drums. Pure Prairie League, however, was plagued by constant personnel changes throughout its history. By the time the band recorded its *Bustin' Out* album in 1975, the group was essentially Fuller and Powell, and a crew of session musicians. For that particular record they enlisted David Bowie alumnus Mick Ronson to add lush string arrangements and scored with "Amie."

At the time Vince joined Pure Prairie League, the group consisted of Michael Connor on keyboards, Billy Hinds on drums, Michael Reilly on bass and vocals, and Jeff Wilson on lead guitar and vocals. At this point, Reilly was the only original member of the band. Although Vince was the new kid in the group, he quickly became its lead vocalist. He also played lead guitar, fiddle, and banjo. A virtual "jack of all trades," this was an excellent opportunity for Gill to polish his musical skills.

While they were preparing to record their first album with Vince Gill aboard, Pure Prairie League played several gigs as a performing band. Because they already had an established following, these performances exposed Gill to a whole new audience, and it brought a whole new audience to him as well.

Although he had just signed to be a part of the biggest band he had ever been associated with to date, the offers for work just kept coming to him. During this same era, Vince's pal Rodney Crowell had been part of Emmylou Harris's backup band. In 1978 Rodney left Harris's group and phoned Vince. He asked Gill to join the new band he was putting together, called the Cherry Bombs. Vince explained that, although he would love to join Rodney, he had just started with Pure Prairie League and that they were presently awaiting the release of their first album with him as a member.

Vince's first album with the group was *Can't Hold Back,* for RCA Records, the band's long-time label. A major highlight on this 1979 release was the title song, "I Can't Hold Back," which was written by Gill. It is an upbeat, pop/rock song with discolike drumming behind Vince's unmistakable voice. The song is propelled by soaring keyboards and guitars, accented by jazz star David Sanborn's sexy sax.

Another classic on this album found Vince sounding very much like Fleetwood Mac on his composition "I Can't Believe," which is probably his first recorded love song to his future wife, Janis. There is also a touching ballad on this disc, with Gill singing about hitchhiking, with Michael Reilly and Patrick Bolen's beautiful background harmonies supporting him. There is also a fifty-eight-second-long instrumental interlude on the album, which Vince wrote and named after his mother, "Jerene."

One of Pure Prairie League's trademarks was their cover artwork by Jeff Wack. Like the group Yes, and their distinctive, instantly identifiable futuristic landscapes by artist Roger Dean, Pure Prairie League's album cover trademark was cowboy western motifs painted by Wack. They always featured a Yosemite Sam-type 1880s prospector with a droopy moustache and a floppy cowboy hat. The front cover of *Can't Hold Back* was meant to look like swimming pool tiles and the trademark prospector is on hand, this time postage-stamp sized. Because the California-based Pure Prairie League recorded *Can't Hold Back* in Miami, Florida, at the famed Criteria Studios, they got to hang out in the sun and enjoy boating while working on the album. This is reflected on the album's back cover where there are four group photos of Pure Prairie League—including Vince Gill—swimming in the Atlantic Ocean and sailing aboard a yacht. Two of the photos on the album show Vince on the deck of a sailing ship, looking very much like the round-faced twenty-one-year-old he was at the time, complete with thick and shaggy shoulder-length brown hair.

The *Can't Hold Back* album contains Vince Gill's earliest recorded lead singing and is a little-known classic in his vast catalog of work. Although the group's music was in the style of what the Doobie Brothers and the Eagles were accomplishing at the time, Pure Prairie League never attained the kind of lasting success that those two institutions have achieved. This particular album, with music by Vince, is well worth seeking out, as none of the cuts from this album appear on the 1995 CD *The Best of Pure Prairie League*. (There are, however, nine Vince Gill cuts that do appear on that CD "hits" collection, taken from his second and third albums with the group.)

The second Pure Prairie League album that Vince performed on was 1980's *Firin' Up*. Although Pure Prairie League had spent the majority of their recording time at RCA Records, after Vince came on board, and after the *Can't Hold Back* album, the band signed a recording deal for two albums on Casablanca Records. Headed by Neil Bogart, Casablanca Records had become world famous for its 1970s disco acts. Not only were Donna Summer and the Village People two of the label's biggest disco acts, but Casablanca also seemed to be the organization that disco put on the map. Its other major talent at the time was the shock rock group KISS.

In an effort to diversify its roster of artists in the late 1970s, Casablanca sought out recording acts that would expand the label's buyer appeal. They signed Cher, who immediately scored with her disco smash "Take Me Home" (1979). The company also contracted the Captain & Tennille, and instantly they experienced one of the biggest hits of their career with "Do That to Me One More Time" (1979).

It was with Vince Gill in the band, and while at Casablanca Records, that Pure Prairie League scored their biggest hit single and the best and largest album sales of their long career as a band. This was also to be the major high point in Vince's career to date. The album was *Firin' Up,* and it contained the very popular "Let Me Love You Tonight," a melodic ballad boasting Vince's expressive lead vocal and showcasing a guest saxophone solo by jazz legend David Sanborn.

During this same era, one of the executives at Casablanca Records was Suzy Frank, who distinctly recalls Pure Prairie League specialness. "It was just refreshing to have them on the label, the kind of music that I really liked," she said to this author in 1998. "At the time, it was the height of the disco era, and the label was very hot with the Village People, the Ritchie Family, Donna Summer, and KISS. Out of the middle of all this came Vince Gill's voice on this beautiful country-style ballad from Pure

Prairie League. It really stood out at the time, especially at Casablanca."

The cover to the *Firin' Up* album featured one of the best of Jeff Wack's portraits of the old cowboy prospector. On this particular layout, the trademark prospector is seated cross-legged at a campfire at sunset. With the moon coming up behind him, he is seen lighting up a hand-rolled cigarette. On the back of the album (and reissue CD interior), there were individual shots of band members Billy Hinds, Michael Connor, Jeff Wilson, Michael Reilly, and Vince Gill. The photo of Vince is very amusing. At this point, his hair was long and hippie-looking. He wore jeans and a white sport jacket over a "UCLA 39" athletic T-shirt. This was the height of Vince's rock star phase, and he was playing it up for all it was worth. The 1970s-style long hair and the grungy looking clothes he had in those days certainly wouldn't lead one to suspect that this same person would become one of the sexiest men in 1990s Nashville.

One of the songs on the *Firin' Up* album, "I'll Be Damned," which was written by Vince, also contains the first recording to feature Sweethearts of the Rodeo, with Janis performing under her new married name: Janis Gill. After their long courtship and several months of living together, Vince had finally won her hand, and they were married not long before the *Firin' Up* album was released in 1980. It was a magical time in Vince's career. He had a new wife, a new band, his first recording deal, and his first hit record.

Looking back on that time from the vantage point of 1991, Vince explained to the music industry publication, *The Gavin Report,* "'Let Me Love You Tonight' [1980] was the biggest hit I had with them—I sang lead on that. There were a few others that charted fairly well: 'I'm Almost Ready' [1980] and 'Still Right Here in My Heart' [1981], but nothing as big as 'Let Me Love You Tonight.' That was a Number One A/C [Adult Contemporary] record."

Thanks to "Let Me Love You Tonight," Vince was suddenly in the winner's circle, and his first taste of recording success felt great.

Now that he was playing with an established rock band, Vince began to plot his course with the group, and in his career in general. Speaking to the *Chicago Tribune* in September 1990, he reflected, "I felt I was going to be the one who could really bridge the gap between pop and country and get rock fans interested in country music." Although it took him longer than he may have expected, in the 1990s he accomplished exactly that. He is the male singer who has gotten many non-country music fans to listen to '90s Nashville, and he has persuaded many hard-core country fans to embrace sensitive ballads and string-laden harmonies.

In 1981, Vince Gill released his third album as the front man for Pure Prairie League. *Something in the Night* is a rockier sound for the band, and Gill sounds great rocking out. Part of the reason for the more rock 'n' roll edge that this offering had was due to the producer they used for the session, Rob Fraboni. They recorded the album entirely at Shangri-La Studios in Malibu, California.

Another artist Rob Fraboni was producing at the time was none other than Bonnie Raitt. After several albums of blues/rock in the 1970s, she too was ready to rock out and was working on her stripped-down-to-basics rock 'n' roll entry *Green Light* (1982). It was a natural evolution for Vince to make a guest appearance on one of Bonnie's songs. You can hear him singing backup vocals to Bonnie on the cut "I Can't Help Myself" on *Green Light*.

Although the *Something in the Night* album didn't do as well as *Firin' Up,* two of the singles became minor hits for Pure Prairie

League. The song "Still Right Here in My Heart" made it to number twenty-eight on the pop chart, and "You're Mine Tonight" peaked at number sixty-eight. On the early 1980 musical chart scene, it was truly a mixed bag from the point of view of style. For example, in 1981 KC & the Sunshine Band, Queen, Blondie, Diana Ross, Michael Jackson, Kenny Rogers, Christopher Cross, and Pink Floyd were all scoring number-one hits on the pop charts. Thus, the field was truly wide-open for different types of music.

Highlights on the group's latest album included Vince and the band rocking out on the song "Something in the Night," as well as Gill leading the beautiful ballad "Tell Me One More Time," which again featured the moody jazz saxophone of David Sanborn. One of the catchiest numbers on this release was Vince's composition "Do You Love Me Truly Julie?" which is pure Vince Gill rock 'n' roll from beginning to end. If Gill ever decided to do a 100 percent high-energy rock album, this cut is a great preview of what he would sound like. Four of the cuts from this album can be found on CD on the 1995 release *The Best of Pure Prairie League.* They are, "Still Right Here in My Heart," "You're Mine Tonight," "Something in the Night," and "Tell Me One More Time." Sweethearts of the Rodeo also sang background vocals on *Something in the Night,* and famed rock pianist Nicky Hopkins can be heard on "Tell Me One More Time."

Because he was part of a rock band, his guitar-playing style, according to Vince, differed from how he now plays on his own current country albums. "When I was in Pure Prairie League, I played rock-'n'-roll-style electric guitar," he explained to *Country Guitar* magazine in mid-1995. "There were certain songs, however, that were heavily influenced by guys like Larry Carlton, Robben Ford, and Lee Ritenour. You know, that sweet 335 [guitar] sound, with lots of bending and sustain[-ed notes]."

Looking back at the group Pure Prairie League from the vantage point of 1991, Vince felt that in many ways they were ahead of their time. They would have fit perfectly into 1990s Nashville, where rock influences and country music seemed to blend seamlessly. Vince believed that had Pure Prairie League existed in the 1990s they could have been one of the biggest acts in Nashville, especially if key member Craig Fuller was part of the lineup.

(A very strong parallel existed between Pure Prairie League and another band that was at the pinnacle of its success in the 1980s, the Doobie Brothers. A decade before, after a streak of hits such as "Black Water" and "Jesus Is Just Alright," the Doobie Brothers, too, went through personnel changes. When Michael McDonald joined the band in the late 1970s, he brought to the group a different voice. He also had a different approach, which worked well within the structure of the band's historic sound. Similarly, for three albums, Vince Gill brought his own distinctive sound to Pure Prairie League.)

It was right after Vince recorded *Something in the Night* (1980) for Pure Prairie League that Janis announced that she had a little surprise for him. As he explained in *Modern Screen's Country* magazine in May 1992: "I quit the group I was in, Pure Prairie League, when I found out my wife was pregnant. So I wound up doing the exact opposite thing that most people do. I quit my job, moved into a more expensive house, and told people, 'We're gonna have a baby!' "

Vince almost immediately contacted his buddy Rodney Crowell and asked if now he could take him up on his offer to join the Cherry Bombs. People thought that Vince was insane. How could he quit an established band with an on-going record deal, to join—from what it appeared to be from the outside—an all-star bar band?

Recalling his phone conversation with Rodney Crowell, Gill told *Country Fever,* "When I quit [Pure Prairie League], I called him up and said, 'If it ever comes up where you need a high harmony singer who plays the guitar, please call.' Then we started playing together and then Rosanne [Cash] needed a guitar player, so I started doing that. On the first rehearsal with them, the music started, and I got goosebumps all over. I said, 'Boy, get hold, get set, because you'll get left real quick!'"

Around this same period of time, Rosanne Cash was on a professional hot streak, having scored three consecutive number-one country hits in 1981 and 1982: "Seven Year Ache," "My Baby Thinks He's a Train," and "Blue Moon with Heartache." The daughter of Johnny Cash and Vivian Liberto, she was married to Rodney Crowell from 1979 to 1992. It was a fascinating time for everyone in this circle of friends who seemed to look out for the others, make music together, and each have their time at bat on the music charts.

Tony Brown was the first keyboard player in Crowell's group. Tony and Vince hit it off immediately. Little did Gill know at the time, but it was Tony Brown who was going to be the singularly most important person in his life as a solo recording star.

Brown told *New Country* magazine in 1996 about the first meeting between the Cherry Bombs and Vince. It was Emory L. Gordy Jr. who brought Vince by the rehearsal sessions for the Cherry Bombs. Tony Brown was startled that regular guitarists Albert Lee and Richard Bennett weren't present. He had been told that Vince used to be with Pure Prairie League, so he was worried that the newcomer was a bit too rock 'n' roll for the sound they needed. "Then I found out he was from Oklahoma and had played in bands with Ricky Skaggs and Keith Whitley," Brown would recall. "I'm sort of starstruck—I'm really intrigued by especially gifted people. So the first thing I was excited about was having a guy like Vince singing harmony behind Rodney [Crowell]. And then he started playing guitar and it floored me—he was as fast as Albert [Lee]!"

Despite the negative feelings he got about this career move, Vince felt it made perfect sense at the time. Vince was very impressed with Rodney Crowell's group, which included Larry London, Emory L. Gordy Jr., Hank DeVito, and Tony Brown. It made the risk worthwhile for Gill. Although the Cherry Bombs never became successful, in March 1991 when reporter Lisa Smith in *The Gavin Report* asked Vince what the favorite band he played with was, he quickly replied, "Musically, I'd say the Cherry Bombs. I played with them for a couple of years on and off. I'll still play with Rodney sometimes, if his guitar player can't make it or whatever."

The country star was later to recall in the liner notes to his 1995 CD *(The Essential Vince Gill)*: "The level of musicianship in Rodney's group was astounding. They knew exactly what they were doing, and if you didn't stay on your toes, they'd lap you quick."

It seemed like every aspect of Vince's life was in transition, even his personal life. On May 5, 1982, in Los Angeles, Janis and Vince Gill became parents of a baby girl they named Jenny. Having left Pure Prairie League and moving on to be part of Rodney Crowell's band left young Vince with much more time to spend with his new little family.

Looking back on this career decision, Vince in the 1990s feels that his strong rapport and close relationship with his daughter Jenny dates back to her first seven years when he was home all of the time. During this era, Gill didn't tour very much at all. This was entirely his own decision.

More than a year went by and Vince was still playing, off and on, in the Cherry Bombs, as well as performing concert dates as part of Rosanne Cash's backup band. At the time, Rosanne and Rodney were a couple, so it seemed like Vince was playing guitar nightly and singing with close friends.

One of the most awesome aspects of being part of Rosanne's band was the fact that Vince was the replacement for recording session guitar player Albert Lee. Albert had long been one of Gill's guitar idols, so to be filling his shoes really amazed him.

Speaking about his favorite guitar legends from this period of musical history, Vince would relate to *Country Guitar* in its Summer 1995 issue: "Of course I listened to Albert Lee and James Burton [Elvis Presley's guitar player]. But I also was enthralled by fusion players such as Larry Carlton and Robben Ford, as well as bluesmen like Eric Clapton. . . . Larry always chooses the perfect notes to play. And his bends are always unpredictable."

It was during this era that Vince began to hit his stride as a country guitar player. He was working with musicians who encouraged him to stretch and define his own unique sound. According to Gill, he was in awe when Rosanne Cash gave him free license to play some of the songs in her stage repertoire with his own personal flair, instead of mimicking his predecessor's (Albert Lee) guitar work lick for lick. It was a tribute to Gill's acknowledged guitar-playing talent.

———•—••—•———

At this point in his career, circa 1980, Vince Gill thought of himself as more of a rock singer than a country singer. His attempts at landing a record deal for himself in Los Angeles, however, were yielding no results. Likewise, Janis Gill's group, Sweethearts of the Rodeo, had yet to garner a recording deal either. They both kept hoping for their lucky break to happen in the record business.

It was Tony Brown who broke the stalemate for Vince. Tony was someone who was literally born into the music business. He was the youngest son in a family of revival-meeting-style performers: the Brown Family Gospel Singers. With his parents (Floyd and Agnes) and his siblings (Henry, Jerry, and Nancy), Tony grew up touring the South and singing religious songs at churches, picnics, and other social gatherings. At the age of thirteen, Tony was enrolled at the Stamps Quartet School of Music in Dallas, Texas, where he learned to play the piano. By the time he was a young adult, Brown had begun playing the keyboards for J. D. Sumner and his famed Stamps Quartet, who were also big on the gospel circuit. The Quartet is best known for its association with Elvis Presley. In the mid-1970s, whenever Presley wanted to hear live gospel music, he would hire J. D. and the quartet to perform for him, privately, in his home. Tony found himself at either Graceland or at one of Elvis's other houses in California at Palm Springs or Los Angeles playing piano for these gospel evenings.

One thing led to another, and before long Tony was playing piano in concert for Presley's opening act, the Sweet Inspirations. Eventually, Tony was to become Elvis's personal keyboard player as well. Suddenly, on August 16, 1977, Elvis died, and Tony found himself without a job. His next paying professional gig was as part of Emmylou Harris's backup band. After that, he moved from Nashville to Los Angeles, where he joined Rodney Crowell's Cherry Bombs. There he met Vince Gill. In 1980 Brown moved back to Nashville when he became the director of the A&R (Artists and Repertoire) department for RCA Records.

It was during this same period, right after Tony Brown made the transition from being a musician to becoming a record industry executive, that he gave his long-time pal Vince Gill one of his biggest career breaks. Because Tony had a great ear for good music, among the first people he thought about signing to the label were his old friends and singing and playing buddies, people he respected as musicians.

"You don't have to live in Nashville to get a record deal in Nashville," Vince explained in *Country Fever* magazine in mid-1994. "That was at a time when techno-pop groups like Devo were the rage, and acoustic guitar-playing singer/songwriters were treated like old news. . . . It was definitely wrong timing there. Tony said, 'Have you thought about making a country record?' He brought the big execs to see me while I was playing guitar with Rosanne [Cash] in Houston, and they signed me just from being her guitar player and harmony singer. So we moved during the holiday season of '83."

Nashville was a thriving place then. After a country music slump in the mid-1970s, the John Travolta/Debra Winger film *Urban Cowboy* (1980) started a country music explosion in the United States and elsewhere. Suddenly country music was hot again, and a whole upsurge of music, money, and excitement was occurring in Nashville. Vince was also very excited that several of his best friends were heading back to Music City as well, including Emmylou Harris and Rodney Crowell. It seemed to Gill like the best place to be.

Vince and Janis loaded themselves and their infant daughter, Jenny, into a rented moving truck and headed for Tennessee. When they arrived there and found the weather to be seventeen degrees below zero, Janis began to wonder what she had been talked into by her enthusiastic husband. Gill, however, was convinced that everything would somehow turn out fine as it always had in the past.

With that, Vince, Janis, and Jenny settled into Nashville living. As they prepared to spend their first Christmas in the legendary city, visions of gold records and country music danced in their heads.

FOUR

TURN ME LOOSE

When Vince Gill first came to RCA Records in 1983, something very ironic happened. The reason that he ended up with a record deal at all was because of Tony Brown. It was surmised that, because Tony had brought him to the label, Brown would be supervising and/or producing Vince's first solo release. Between Gill's signing the contract and entering the recording studio, however, Brown was offered the job of heading MCA Records' Nashville division, and off he went to his new assignment. Thus, instead of having Tony Brown as producer, Emory L. Gordy Jr. took the helm for Gill's debut recording project at RCA.

In the early 1980s, RCA Records signed several new country artists to their label, and instead of releasing a full album of eight to twelve cuts, they recorded and released six-song, full-sized, twelve-inch vinyl discs, selling them at a lower price and marketing them as "Extended Play" singles, known as EPs. In this way, they could launch new acts with a relatively minimal expense both to the record company and to the record buyer. Among the artists whose debut album was an EP, as opposed to an LP (Long Play), were the Judds and Vince Gill.

Vince's debut EP was released in 1984. Entitled *Turn Me Loose*, four of the songs were the artist's own compositions: "Turn Me Loose," "Don't Say That You Love Me," "Half a Chance," and "'Til the Best Comes Along." Also on the EP were Delbert McClinton's "Victim of Life's Circumstances," and "Oh Carolina," which was written by Randy Albright, Jim Elliot, and Mark D. Sanders. Years later, in 1994, when *Turn Me Loose* was reissued on CD, two additional Gill compositions, "Waitin' for Your Love" and "Livin' the Way I Do," were included to expand it into a full eight-cut offering.

Reviewing the *Turn Me Loose* disc, critic Jim Worbois in *All Music Guide to Country* (1997) wrote: "While Gill had been on the musical scene for several years including a stint with Pure Prairie League, this is a nice sampler to display Gill's skills as both a performer and a writer."

Recalls singer/songwriter Carl Jackson in the book *Hot Country* (1993): "I didn't really know Gill that well until that first little mini-LP he did on RCA, which I sang harmony on. Emory Gordy produced it and Emory was a friend and he called and asked me if I would sing harmony on it, and I had heard about Vince and was more than happy to do it, and then, after hearing those sides that Emory had done, I mean, he [Vince] just blew me away—his vocal ability and his playing ability."

Although *Turn Me Loose* did not exactly have soaring sales figures, it did yield Vince's first single hit, "Victim of Life's Circumstances." One step at a time, he was about to start establishing his name in the country music realm.

One of the brightest things that happened during Vince's RCA years (1983–89) came when the Academy of Country Music named him the "1984 New Male Vocalist of the Year." It was a brilliant confirmation that Gill was on the right track with his music.

As soon as Vince had arrived in Nashville, he wasted no time immersing himself in the music and the flavor of all that the city had to offer. He began networking almost instantly, hanging out with old friends, and establishing new contacts. One of his prime methods was to play guitar and sing behind other performers, just to get his feet wet in the clubs and recording studios of country music's Music City.

This was to establish a lifelong pattern for Vince, totally separate from his RCA recording contract, and, later, apart from his solo recording career with MCA. There was no major record company sponsoring a tour for him at the time, and he was free to do as much session work on other people's records as he wanted. That was exactly what he did then and continues to do to this present day. He simply loves to make music and does so whenever possible.

One of the first places at which Vince Gill publicly performed in Nashville was the Bluebird Café. Located at 4104 Hillsboro Road, the venue had opened originally in 1982 as a casual restaurant which also happened to feature music. Operated by Amy Kurland, on Sunday nights the Bluebird Café has a special songwriter's showcase, where unknown performers could perform their songs and, hopefully, find someone interested in either publishing or recording them. (When the 1993 movie *The Thing Called Love* was shot in Nashville, starring River Phoenix and Sandra Bullock, the Bluebird Café was used in that movie's plotline. K. T. Oslin portrayed a fictional version of Amy in that picture directed by Peter Bogdanovich. Trisha Yearwood was also featured in this fascinating look at hopefuls in 1990s Nashville.)

In her two decades of running the club, Kurland has seen many of the hottest country stars come into her establishment when they were only unknowns. According to Amy in *Playgirl* magazine (August 1998): "Every once in a while someone who really impresses me will come along on a Sunday night. When Garth [Brooks] auditioned for a Sunday writer's night, I remember scribbling 'good voice' on the application. . . . Vince Gill played the café for the first time [sitting in] with David Grisman and a band called Here Today, and we had a huge crowd because they had just finished making an album with Dan Fogelberg. Since Vince [had just moved] to Nashville, David asked me to look after him and help him out once he got settled. It was sure nice to be asked to take him under my wing."

Another project that Vince became involved in at the time was Emmylou Harris's *The Angel Band*. Originally, it was a concept album with Harris gathering together several of her friends and recording country gospel songs. A dozen songs were cut, including "Where Could I Go but to the Lord," "Precious Memories," "Someday My Ship Will Sail," and "When They Ring Those Golden Bells." It was produced by Emory L. Gordy Jr. and Emmylou Harris, and featured a roster of up-and-coming Nashville talent. *The Angel Band* included Emmylou Harris on vocals and guitar; Vince Gill on guitar, mandolin, and vocals; Carl Jackson on guitar and vocals; Emory L. Gordy Jr. on bass, guitar, and vocals; and Mark O'Connor on fiddle, viola, and mandola. *The Angel Band* did not get released by Warner Bros. until 1987, although it had been recorded several years before, right after Vince had moved to Nashville. It is a little-known acoustic masterpiece well worth discovering.

Emmylou Harris was just one of dozens of solo performers on whose recordings Vince has appeared over the years. Whenever he has the chance to sing or play guitar on anyone's recording session—he is right there to lend a guitar or a tenor voice. In this way, he is expanding his musical scope, his reputation, and his wallet. To date, Gill can also be heard on albums by Bonnie Raitt, Reba McEntire, Conway Twitty, Patty Loveless, Emmylou Harris, and the rock group Dire Straits. There was even a point at which Mark Knopfler of Dire Straits tried to convince Vince to join his band. Gill, however, had his sights on his first shot at a solo career at RCA Records.

Bonnie Raitt and Emmylou Harris were two of the people who returned the favor when Vince began recording for RCA, both lending their voices to his recordings. According to Vince in *Country Fever* magazine (February 1993): "I would say I've learned a lot from Emmy. She's a very unselfish person. If she's got the time and all that, she'll sing. She sang with me when I was getting started, and I love her to death for that." On the *Turn Me Loose* EP in 1983, Emmylou can be heard on "Oh Carolina," which is one of the best songs from his much-ignored RCA era.

In retrospect, this post-Pure Prairie League mid-1980s period is looked on as a slow time for Vince Gill's solo career. In reality, however, he placed eleven different singles in the Country Top Forty posted in *Billboard* magazine, three of them were contained on the *Turn Me Loose* EP and charted in 1984. His first single, "Victim of Life's Circumstances" charted at number forty, followed by "Oh Carolina" peaking at number thirty-eight, followed by "Turn Me Loose," which hit number thirty-nine.

At the time Vince wasn't certain if he should even be marketed as a country singer. According to him years later in *Country Weekly* in February 1999: "As far as my style, I have some traditional country roots and some modern roots in my music. . . . They put the country label on it because it comes from Nashville and I come from Oklahoma. It would be nice if people got away from labels—branding the music seems to limit it."

Gill was especially frustrated by country radio at the time. As he explained for *Country Weekly* in 1999: "I couldn't seem to get noticed in the mid-1980s. They only play[ed] Kenny [Rogers], only Dolly [Parton], only Alabama, only proven performers. With new artists, there's the fear: 'Dare we play this new thing? Somebody might not like it and tune us out.'"

In spite of airplay problems, Vince's debut disc on RCA provided his solo career with a fitting start. Upon listening to this debut solo release, you can hear a singing legend in the making. Beginning with the title cut, "Turn Me Loose," it is a total rock 'n' roll song, which sounds totally in line with the photos used on this six-cut EP. On the front cover, Vince is wearing a purple shirt and a turquoise jacket, and a hot pink spotlight is lighting the right side of his face. On the back cover, Gill is shown in a full-length body shot, playing his guitar on a checkered floor against an ultraviolet backdrop. One would think that this was more of a Duran Duran album than a country release.

The album's "Oh Carolina," which features Emmylou Harris singing the harmony vocals behind him, takes the release more toward a folk/country bent. This is the first in a long series of songs that Vince has done that are about Southern states and cities which are also women's names. [This list also includes "Hills of Carolina" and "Savannah (Don't You Ever Think of Me)."] The third song, "Don't Say That You Love Me," is another rock 'n' roll number, which Vince co-wrote with Emory L. Gordy Jr., and contains background vocals by Vince and his wife, Janis. At the time, her singing career had come to a temporary halt, as she was spending most of her time at home as a wife, mother, and homemaker.

The second side of Vince's mini-album opens with "Half a Chance." It features Hank DeVito's crying pedal steel guitar and is more of a country ballad with a nice Texas dancehall feeling to it. The next song, "Victim of Life's Circumstances," was written by Delbert McClinton, the great Texas singer/songwriter, who would later win a Grammy Award for the 1991 duet "Good Man/Good Woman" with Bonnie Raitt. "Victim" is an upbeat country rocker about a musician on his way to Memphis, who ends up in jail for rowdiness. The sixth song on this disc is the slow ballad, "'Til the Best Comes Along," written by Gill. A song of modest resignation,

Vince goes for a slow dancing tempo and makes this a memorable and insightful tune.

The original vinyl version of *Turn Me Loose* featured liner notes written by Rosanne Cash and Rodney Crowell, which read: "Musically, Vince is what you'd call a true triple threat, in that he writes songs that will make you cry, he sings like everyday is payday, and he can play the hell out of a guitar. . . . We are very pleased to call Vince our friend and have his music be a part of our lives, and we'll bet you, the record-buying public, that once you've had a taste of Vince Gill's music, [you] won't want to ever turn it loose."

Vince's sense of humor on this album is subtlely displayed on the liner notes. On the song "Oh Carolina," the musicians credits are listed, and the last one reads: "Phil Kaufman—Babysitting." Well, when both mom and dad are in the music business, someone has to watch baby Jenny Jerene Gill in the recording studio while they make music!

In 1985 Vince released his first full-length solo album for RCA, *The Things That Matter*. Again he chose his friend Emory L. Gordy Jr. to produce it. Gill pulled four hit singles from this album. His composition "True Love" made it to number thirty-two when it was released in the spring of 1985. It was, however, "If It Weren't for Him" with Rosanne Cash providing guest vocals that made it to number ten in the middle of that same year. He followed it with "Oklahoma Borderline," which hit number nine. Written by Vince, Rodney Crowell, and Guy Clark, that recording also features Crowell and Herb Pedersen singing in the background. Unfortunately, Gill couldn't maintain the same momentum on his next single. Released in July 1986, "With You," taken from this same album, peaked at number thirty-three.

Meanwhile, Vince wasn't the only Gill in the household to have things heat up in their career. In 1985 there was to be a singing contest held in Nashville. Janis had convinced her sister Kristine to join her there and enter Sweethearts of the Rodeo into the competition. The live talent show that they signed up for was the Wrangler Country Showdown Talent Contest—and they won first prize!

Vince believed it was a sign that Janis and Kristine deserved a break. He loved their music, but they had never reached prominence, primarily because they could not get their own recording deal. Although Gill didn't have a lot of clout in town, he took matters into his own hands to get them signed. He took their tapes to the head of A&R at the CBS label, Bonnie Gardner. Soon, CBS signed the duo to a recording contract.

The self-titled *Sweethearts of the Rodeo* debut album came out in 1986, containing only eight cuts. Four of those were released as singles, with three of them landing in country music Top Ten in *Billboard* magazine. Their first single, "Hello Doll Baby," was a remake of the Clovers 1956 R&B hit, and it made it all the way to number twenty-one. When "Since I Found You" was released in the summer of 1986, it bolted all the way up to number seven. They followed it with "Midnight Girl/Sunset Town" in December 1986 and "Chains of Gold" in April 1987, and both of them rose to number four. In fact, this was just the beginning of the hits for Sweethearts of the Rodeo. Between 1986 and 1989 they racked up seven consecutive Top Ten singles, which far eclipsed the modest success that Vince was having at RCA.

Almost instantly, the media, and several people who were looking in from the outside, perceived that there may have been some degree of animosity on Vince's side. Including his three albums with Pure Prairie League, Vince was five LPs into his career, while his wife and sister-in-law jump in and have the phenomenal success that he had always wanted.

From that point on, it became a game of "he said"/"she said" between moderately successful Vince and very successful Janis. The press seemed to emphasize the opinion that Gill couldn't help but be jealous of his wife's "overnight" success on the record charts, while his own releases languished. In March 1991 Vince said in *The Gavin Report* magazine: "I guess you'll hear all kinds of things, and Janis probably has a whole different side of our relationship than I do. When the Sweethearts started taking off, I think she saw it the wrong way, that I was envious of her success and I was hard on her because of it. I really wasn't. . . . I didn't begrudge her success. A lot of people put the term success on how your recording career does. Mine was not explosive, but I was doing so many other things that were just as gratifying to me. Nobody else understood that."

In retrospect Gill proclaimed in *Modern Screen's Country* magazine in its Fall 1991 issue: "I was never bitter. I might have been frustrated and maybe I took it out on her a little, but not intentionally. I've always been real proud of her."

From her perspective, Janis explained in *People* magazine earlier that same year: "I would say the most problems we had was when my career was taking off, because it happened so quickly. I was being pulled in a million different directions, and it was tough getting into the rhythm and the rhyme of a life like that. That's upsetting to a household, especially when your husband is trying to do the same thing. . . . I used to pray for hits for him, because he deserves it. But past that point, I really knew it would help [our marriage]."

Vince explained in *Country Fever* magazine in mid-1994: "My makeup is not that I have to be the star, the front man, the lead singer or have hits. . . . Janis might tell you different, and I might be an idiot here, but I don't think that way in a majority of cases. I'm sure I have a little bit of that male ego that has been passed down from generations, but it was that I was still earning a good deal of money. If you want to talk strictly financial or strictly creatively . . . with all the session work I was doing, I was doing fine."

According to Vince, he was never overly concerned that his career would never peak. He realized that making hit records was not the only way he could earn a good living in Nashville. He was ready, willing, and able to be a recording session guitar player, or a touring guitar player, with just about any of the headliners in town. At the time he made an impressive amount of money as a harmony singer and a background vocalist on the recordings of several other artists. Although some observers perceived this as Vince being less than ambitious with his own career, for him it was just as impressive and important to sing behind an established star like Conway Twitty, as it was to create his own recordings.

This wasn't an uncommon occurrence in Nashville. For example, Marty Stuart, Ricky Skaggs, and Mark O'Connor are all names you can find listed in the liner notes of 1980s and 1990s albums by dozens and dozens of other stars. Like Gill, even after they became headliners in their own right, they continued to lend their voices and/or their musicianship to the recordings of other Nashville performers.

Christmas 1986 provided Vince with one of his fondest holiday memories with his young daughter. According to Gill in *Country Weekly* (December 2, 1996): "Jenny and I went out shopping for the tree when she was about three. The catch was she had to carry it home! So we bought this little bitty sweet tree and put a couple of lights on it and that was pretty sickly. It was neat because she didn't want to have the biggest, most beautiful tree; she wanted to carry it." It provided a Christmas season that Vince would always remember.

Finally, in 1987, on his third solo album, *The Way Back Home*, things started to pick up professionally for Gill. In fact, *The Way*

Back Home disc has such a nice varied feeling to it and is so nicely packaged that it really deserves to be released as a CD just the way it appeared originally. The cover has a good shot of Vince at his most svelte, in a red shirt and a plaid jacket, against a vibrant orange urban sunset. The album opens at a full-tilt rhythmic pace with the tongue-in-cheek song about his wife, "Everybody's Sweetheart." He follows it with his composition about runaway children, "The Way Back Home," which features background vocals by Emmylou Harris and Bonnie Raitt. With references to lost youngsters trying to find their way home, this touching ballad is a beautiful early example of Vince the storyteller.

"Cinderella," the third song on this album represents the first time that Vince sang a song written by Reed Nielsen, who was destined to become one of Gill's top collaborators in the 1990s. This medium-tempo song is light and catchy, about a forlorn rags-to-riches girl. The upbeat "Let's Do Something" and the clever "The Radio" represent the artist's earliest collaborations with Nielsen. (Vince's writing with Nielsen later yielded such 1990s classics as "Don't Come Cryin' to Me" and "You Better Think Twice.")

The second side of this album opens with "Baby That's Tough," with do-wop style background vocals that sound like the Jordanaires, who used to sing behind Elvis Presley. "Losing Your Love" is a classic Vince Gill sad ballad, which he was getting good at writing and have been a staple of his lengthy career. "It Doesn't Matter Anymore" is an interesting cover song for Gill to do on this album. Written by Paul Anka, this is the first of two numbers Vince has recorded that were done earlier by Linda Ronstadt on her *Heart Like a Wheel* (1974) album. The ninth and last cut on Gill's *The Way Back Home* is "Something's Missing," which he wrote with Michael Clark. It is a rock ballad about a lost love, sounding very much like an Eagles tune from the 1970s.

All in all, *The Way Back Home* is a solid showcase of the many musical sides of Vince Gill. With his handsome photo on the cover, a brilliant supporting cast, well-crafted songs, and consistently good singing, this is definitely his best album package from his RCA days.

According to country music writer Alanna Nash, in *Stereo Review* magazine in 1987: "In his two previous albums, hotshot singer/songwriter and instrumentalist Vince Gill has sounded like a slave to his influences, notably Rodney Crowell, Rosanne Cash, and Emmylou Harris. In his third album, however, Gill crafts his songs as if he might be trying to find his own sound, with the sweet irony that the new record employs those same aforementioned progressive country soulmates. . . . *The Way Back Home* amounts to a sampler of varying styles—all winning and enormously engaging—that Gill is still trying on. One of them, one day, may also furnish a sense of identity."

Finally in the spring of 1987, Vince scored another Top Ten hit with "Cinderella," which peaked at number five. The song had a nice country bluegrass flavor to it, complete with fiddle, banjo, and mandolin. It was something of a "reunion" recording for him, as the fiddle playing on that entry was provided by his former employer, Byron Berline. Over the next year, Gill released three subsequent Top Forty singles: "Let's Do Something," which made it to number sixteen; "Everybody's Sweetheart," which peaked at number eleven; and finally "The Radio," which froze at number thirty-nine.

Two of these songs, "The Radio" and "Everybody's Sweetheart," were written and sung by Vince, about his wife, Janis. "The Radio" concerns someone missing his lover, yet he is able to hear her voice over the airwaves because she is a successful star. "Everybody's Sweetheart" obviously pokes fun at Janis's group name, and in the lyrics, he teases about how she is everybody's sweetheart—but his.

In 1988 Vince went across the Atlantic Ocean for his first European tour. While he was performing there, he wrote the song "I Never Knew Lonely," to describe how he felt at the time, missing his family. When he came back to America, Gill went into the studio with RCA producer Barry Beckett and recorded this number.

"I Never Knew Lonely" became something of a transition song for him. His contract with RCA Records was up in 1989. Tony Brown was again offering Vince a recording deal. This time around it was to be at the company with which Brown was now associated, MCA Records.

When it was clear that Vince was definitely going on to a bigger career at MCA, just to capitalize upon the great material he had recorded already for RCA, that label released *The Best of Vince Gill.* It included the newly recorded "I Never Knew Lonely," seven of his Top Forty singles, and two previously unreleased songs, "Lucy Dee" and "I've Been Hearing Things About You."

Vince was understandably unhappy with his failure during the RCA period to connect with a strong audience or to establish a consistently strong music chart presence. Was it something to do with the quality of the music, or with Vince's singing? "I thought I was pretty good," he said to the *Los Angeles Times* a few years later in September 1994. "I felt like I belonged. I knew I could play and I knew I could sing. I didn't mean that egotistically. My ears tell me that, that I have some talent. And I love it. I mean music is the greatest thing in my life."

True to his easygoing nature, he refused to complain publicly about RCA's handling of his recording career. Vince was ready to move on to greener pastures, and like he has always done, he never once looked back.

After his departure from RCA Records, the label packaged and repackaged his solo recordings from this era repeatedly, overlapping the most obvious songs over and over again, disc to disc. Although they have shuffled them many ways, to date there still isn't a Vince Gill compact disc that contains all of his Top Forty recordings from this period. The song "If It Weren't for Him" is constantly overlooked on these re-packagings. In addition, they all feature less than complete liner notes. One of the best RCA compilations is *The Essential Vince Gill* (1995). It contains twenty songs and surveys the widest variety of the star's recordings for RCA. Also of note is the eight-cut disc *Vince Gill and Friends* (1998), which features Vince singing with Bonnie Raitt, Emmylou Harris, Rodney Crowell, and Sweethearts of the Rodeo. It is the only RCA CD package to date that lists any of the singers track by track.

In 1992, RCA released the album *I Never Knew Lonely*, which featured the previously unreleased songs "What If I Say Goodbye" and "Midnight Train." *Vince Gill: Super Hits*, which was distributed in 1996, is also worth seeking out, as it contains the hard-to-find cuts "Losing Your Love," "Savannah (Don't You Ever Think of Me)," and "Baby That's Tough." Another one worth checking out is *Vintage Gill—The Encore Collection* (1997). It contains the rarely heard "'Til the Best Comes Along," as well as "Baby That's Tough."

When Vince made the move to MCA Records in 1989, he brought to the table ten years of experience in the record business. Including "Let Me Love You Tonight" with Pure Prairie League, Vince had recorded four Top Ten hits, six albums, and a greatest hits package. Unknown to him at the time, he was on the threshold of his greatest solo recording success.

FIVE

WHEN I CALL YOUR NAME

In 1989, at the same time that Vince Gill made his switch to the MCA record label, his career wasn't the only thing that was suddenly accelerating. Nashville and the whole face of country music was beginning to change drastically and very quickly. In the 1970s, there was a domination of the industry sales charts by the old guard of Nashville—people such as Johnny Cash, Hank Williams Jr., and Conway Twitty. In the 1980s, Alabama came along and proved that a country/rock band could rule the charts. Also, the "New Traditionalists" movement started, with Randy Travis, Dwight Yoakam, and George Strait bringing the classic sounds of 1950s and 1960s rockabilly, swing, and western elements back to country.

In the 1990s, there was suddenly a fresh influx of new stars in Music City. There was fresh talent, new energy, and a whole new generation of music buyers who didn't have a clue who such genre veterans as Waylon Jennings or Mel Tillis were. Many of the changes in Nashville came about because of country music television networks such as TNN (the Nashville Network), CMT (Country Music Television), and eventually GAC (Great American Country). Just like MTV (which focused on the area of rock music) had demanded in the 1980s, suddenly country music stars had to be young and fresh and sexy looking. Not only did they have to sound good on record, but they had to look hot on video while they sang their hits.

All of a sudden "country hunks" such as Clint Black, Alan Jackson, Travis Tritt, Marty Stuart, Aaron Tippin, Billy Dean, and Brooks & Dunn were all the rage. On the other side of the coin, country gals such as Lorrie Morgan, Reba McEntire, Holly Dunn, Suzy Bogguss, and Trisha Yearwood gave the music of Nashville a sexy new appeal. As the demographics for country music listeners suddenly got younger and younger, the door was left wide open for the likes of teenage stars such as Bryan White and LeAnn Rimes.

Among the number-one songs on the *Billboard* Hot Country Singles chart in 1989 were established stars and hits including: Dolly Parton's "Why'd You Come in Here Lookin' Like That," Willie Nelson's "Nothing I Can Do About it Now," Randy Travis's "It's Just a Matter of Time," the Judds' "Change of Heart," Alabama's "If I Had You," Rosanne Cash's "I Don't Want to Spoil the Party," and Rodney Crowell's "After All This Time." They were joined at the top of the sales charts that year by several newcomers, including: Garth Brooks's "If Tomorrow Never Comes," Clint Black's "Better Man," and Patty Loveless's "Timber, I'm Falling in Love."

With the new wave of country music came a rewesternization of the country music image as well. In the 1970s it was all big hair for the ladies (Tammy Wynette, Loretta Lynn, Lynn Anderson) and spandex and spangles for everyone. In the 1990s, however, the look of the cowboy and the cowgirl were reintroduced to Nashville. With that came the "hat acts." Men in Stetson cowboy hats and skin tight jeans were all the rage. In that category came Garth Brooks, Brooks & Dunn, Tracy Lawrence, Mark Chesnutt, George Strait, Joe Diffie, and Tim McGraw, to name a few. Almost instantly, great country music also had to be accompanied with a great image and a great video to catapult it to the top.

In addition to all that, the subjects covered by country music singers were suddenly widening. What used to be a bunch of "I lost my job," "I lost my lover," "I lost my dog" songs, and "let's go get drunk" songs was replaced by catchy tunes and intelligent lyrics. Insightful singer/songwriters such as Mary Chapin Carpenter, Garth Brooks, and Pam Tillis were suddenly in vogue as well.

Into this atmosphere of revitalized Nashville, Vince Gill changed record labels, and everything instantly seemed like a fresh beginning for him. From 1989 to 1991 his career was on a slow but steady build in the country music realm. He wasn't an instant overnight success, but again and again he hit the Top Ten on the country charts. He sang appealingly harmonic songs about life and love, which captured the hearts of record buyers and concert audience members across the country. And, the fact that he was incredibly handsome certainly made him a prime target for 1990s country music superstardom.

The most ironic thing that happened along the way, however, was that as Vince Gill's star rose to Olympian heights in the 1990s, the success of Sweethearts of the Rodeo's records slipped just as quickly off the music charts. In the late 1980s, their string of seven Top Ten hits in a row had continued with "Gotta Get Away" (1987), "Satisfy You" (1988), "Blue to the Bone" (1988), and "I Feel Fine" (1989). They were to experience two more Top Forty successes: "If I Never See Midnight Again" (1990) and "This Heart" (1990), but after that, they seemed to disappear from the public eye. Regardless of genre, the music business is very fickle, and the public's fascination with country girl groups seemed to wane. During this same period, the Forester Sisters (number-one hits included "I Fell in Love Again Last Night," 1985, and "You Again," 1987), the Judds, and the country all-star trio of Linda Ronstadt, Emmylou Harris, and Dolly Parton—along with Sweethearts of the Rodeo, made tight female harmonies all the rage on the 1980s' country music charts. As the 1990s approached, however, Nashville was shifting its gears again.

There are many probable reasons why Vince Gill's musical career was sluggish in the 1980s and then explosive in the 1990s. Among the factors that helped him out in this expansion of his career were timing, sound and stronger writing, great looks, the push of one of the most successful record labels in Nashville (MCA), and Vince finally getting to work with his perfectly matched producer, Tony Brown. "He's the reason I went to MCA," Gill clearly stated in the *Gavin Report* in March 1991.

When it came time to record his debut solo album with MCA, Vince Gill pulled out the stops in star power. Singing duets or harmony vocals with him on the *When I Call Your Name* album in 1989 was an all-celebrity cast of costars including Reba McEntire, Patty Loveless, Emmylou Harris, and Kathie Baillie of the group Baillie & the Boys.

Of them all, one of the strongest connections Gill made was with his friendship and collaborative relationship with Patty Loveless. A distant cousin of country legends Loretta Lynn and Crystal Gayle, in 1989 Loveless married Vince's buddy and ex-producer Emory L. Gordy Jr., and her career began to blossom.

When Patty recorded her song "Timber, I'm Falling in Love," Vince came into the studio and provided harmony vocals behind her. The song became her big breakthrough single, and her first recording to hit number one. Returning the favor, when Gill recorded "When I Call Your Name" for his new album, Patty sang it with him. When it was released as a single in 1990, it hit number two on the charts and won the Country Music Association Award as the Single of the Year. As witnessed on both of these hit singles, their voices blended together beautifully and their friendship and work together in concert and on records continues to this day.

When asked at what point his career suddenly came together, without hesitation, Vince Gill replied in the Summer 1995 issue of *Country Guitar* magazine: "It happened in 1989, when I wrote 'When I Call Your Name.' At first, that song was just kind of lying there, collecting dust. It was only when we put Patty Loveless's vocal part on it that, all of a sudden, it became very special. Before that moment, I'd been recording country music for about seven years, and I never could get anything going. It was a struggle to get that first break-through hit. And as we were finishing 'When I Call Your Name,' I said to myself that, 'This is country music the way I hear it. It's who I am, and if it doesn't work, I'll quit.' Fortunately, it did work." Patty Loveless likewise loves and respects Vince. She has stated several times that she considers his voice to be one of the greatest ones around.

Another one of his biggest supporters was the undisputed country queen of MCA Records, Reba McEntire. As a fellow Oklahoman, it seemed like a perfect musical marriage to put them together on the same record. Vince penned the song "Oklahoma Swing," which the two of them turned into a delightful singing romp, displaying a much more playful approach to a number than anything he had done on RCA. Gill was overwhelmingly grateful to McEntire for her kind gesture.

Without a doubt, *When I Call Your Name* is one of the best albums of Vince's entire career. Cut for cut, it is a marvelous showcase for his singing and songwriting. This album also contains three of the strongest ballads he has ever written: "Never Alone," "Never Knew Lonely," and the title song—all of which became hit singles.

There was also a very concentrated effort to craft this MCA album with a very clean traditional country sound. The lonesome pedal steel guitar sounds on "We Could Have Been," the hoedown fun of "Oklahoma Swing," the western flavor of "Ridin' the

Rodeo," and the two-stepping beat of "Rita Ballou" are all fitting country touches to the album. Having completed *When I Call Your Name*, Vince felt that it was the first genuine country record he had ever made, and he was very proud of the results.

At times in the album he even threw in a bit of bluegrass as well. "Sometimes in the harmonies. The backgrounds for 'When I Call Your Name' were straight out bluegrass even though the song itself wasn't. There's an older record of mine called 'Cinderella' that sounds like the Beach Boys meet Bill Monroe. You learn a little from everyone," Vince said in the Fall 1991 *Modern Screen's Country* magazine.

For Gill the recording process was half of the fun. He especially enjoyed working with his pals, singing duets and background parts on his albums. When he wanted a warm male harmony voice that blended well with his, he chose Rodney Crowell. For close female harmony, he selected Reba McEntire and Emmylou Harris. Having his friends involved in the recording of this landmark album in his career meant a lot to Vince.

The press reviews of the album instantly pegged him as a star to watch. *Music City News* asked, concerning Gill's new release: "What do you have when you combine a dazzling vocal ability, a blazing guitar style, and a songwriting gift of immense proportions?" And, Jack Hurst of the *Chicago Tribune* judged at the time: "After six years in Nashville, a man who has sung backup on the records of more than 100 other artists finally has a mega-hit of his own to his credit."

A lot of the credit for the sound on *When I Call Your Name* goes to producer Tony Brown. He arranged for the best musicians he could round up for the recording sessions, made certain that the pacing was kept exciting and varied, and showcased Vince's voice with a focus that his RCA recordings seemed to lack. After all, the material Gill had recorded at RCA did not have the crispness, the sparkle, and the excitement that his first album at MCA contained. Whatever the answer to his new-found success was, there was no doubt that he had truly arrived.

When they first started working together, Tony had no idea how talented Vince really was. According to Brown, several people in Nashville, including himself, took Gill's guitar playing for granted. It wasn't until they teamed together in the recording studio that Brown came to realize how proficient a picker he really was.

Another key to Vince's new-found success was his ability to select duet partners, harmony singers, and background singers to fill in the sound on his recordings. Regarding his rationale for making his costarring vocalist selections, Gill said at the time in the *Gavin Report:* "I wait until the very end to decide who's going to sing on the cuts with me. I feel more like a casting director at that point than a record maker. It's got to be the right voice for the song. But you know their voices, and you know which ones will sound great on what cuts. People always ask me, 'How did you get all those people to sing on your records?' And I tell them to look on the backs of those people's records and ask them the same question."

Vince was the first to admit that during his tenure at RCA he was experimenting with different sounds and song styles. According to him in the *Los Angeles Times* (September 24, 1994): "Creatively I wanted to make records the way I like 'em. . . . It was just [that] nobody wanted to hear it for a while. That was OK."

Big things were starting to happen professionally for Vince. His first single off the album, "Never Alone," was released in the fall of 1989, and peaked at number twenty-two. His duet with Reba, "Oklahoma Swing," made it to number thirteen. Furthermore, the two strongest ballads, "When I Call Your Name" and "Never Knew Lonely," reached number two and number three, respectively. Suddenly, it was Vince Gill who was the new man to watch in Nashville. When the CMA presented Vince with its Single of the Year Award for "When I Call Your Name," he knew that he was on the right path at last. To top it all off, the album *When I Call Your Name* was certified double platinum for more than two million copies sold.

In 1990, at the Academy of Country Music Awards ceremony, Vince and Reba's duet of "Oklahoma Swing" was up against Sweethearts of the Rodeo and the Judds. Fortunately, the Judds won the trophy, thus averting World War III in the Gill household.

Janis Gill claimed in *People* magazine (June 10, 1991): "When you're both on the charts, you're competing with each other and you can imagine what that does to a household."

One of the most exciting aspects of 1991 was when the array of awards and trophies started rolling in for Vince. He said at the time in the *Gavin Report*: "I got nominated for two Grammys and that's real exciting. It'll be the first time I've been to the Grammys. But I really don't set goals to speak of. I just enjoy life and let it unfold like it's going to."

That year, on February 20, he went home with his first Grammy Award in the category of Best Country Vocal, Male, for the song "When I Call Your Name." This was just the beginning of his incredible Grammy Award winning streak throughout the 1990s, as he has won one or more Grammy Awards every single year of the decade from that point onward.

In addition, the list of prizes Vince acquired that year just kept escalating. The BMI Songwriter's Awards honored him with their 1991 Most Performed Songs Awards for "When I Call Your Name," "Oklahoma Swing," and "Never Knew Lonely." The TNN/*Music City News* Awards named him their 1991 Instrumentalist of the Year, and their 1991 Single of the Year was "When I Call Your Name."

Vince's success that year was partly due to the tireless concert tour and record promoting that took place around the United

States. He was now traveling so much that he felt he was rarely at home. At an April 1991 songwriter's awards show, Gill was up on stage, and when he looked out into the audience, he saw his eight-year-old daughter, Jenny, staring up at him. Because that was the first time he had laid eyes on her in two months, he was brought to tears by that touching moment. "It stirred up a bunch of emotions," Vince admitted in the June 10, 1991, issue of *People* magazine. "I know there are a lot of times she'd come home and I wouldn't be there."

The *When I Call Your Name* album was an instant success from the moment it was released and went on to sell more than two million copies. Almost immediately it became clear that MCA Records was 100 percent behind Vince and his debut disc on the label. In addition to the impressive sales figures, the music industry awards that he won during this period were an undeniable sign that he was finally on the right career path.

Vince's enthusiasm was one of the most exciting things to see as he began collecting one trophy after another in the 1990s. In 1990, when Gill won the CMA Award for "When I Call Your Name," he received a standing ovation. According to him, it was one of the most rewarding moments in his entire professional life.

Meanwhile, his recording career was off and running. Continuing to perform on other people's records whenever he could, in 1991 Vince was heard on Nashville session musician Mark O'Connor's *New Nashville Cats* album on the cut "Restless." Gill was one of the three guest vocalists on the song—including Steve Wariner and Ricky Skaggs—billed as the *New Nashville Cats*.

At the same time, it was back in the studio for Vince to record his second album for MCA: *Pocket Full of Gold* (1991). According to Gill, he deliberately aimed to have a more unified country theme to the songs used in the release and to include a more country-oriented approach to the music itself.

Now bouncing back and forth from lonely blues ballads such as "Look at Us," popish "Liza Jane," and the giddy-up tempo "Sparkle," the singing star was the first to admit that he was tackling several different styles in his new albums.

Vince's *Pocket Full of Gold* opens with fiddles and steel guitar wailing on the song "I Quit," making this one of the liveliest beginnings to any of his discs to date. In the lyrics of this song, Gill is telling his lover to take a hike. Leading right into the slow and somber hit "Look at Us," again steel guitars and fiddle guide Gill into a song, which is about a true love surviving against all odds. On the next number, "Take Your Memory with You," someone is leaving him. In the first three songs Vince walks out, Vince stays, and then the lover walks out. Obviously this is a country album.

The title song, "Pocket Full of Gold," is very reminiscent of one of Patsy Cline's very first hits in the 1950s, "A Poor Man's Roses or a Rich Man's Gold," the moral of both being that money can't buy you love. Gill's "The Strings That Tie You Down" is a beautiful song about someone about to break up a romance and walk out the door.

The biggest hit on Vince's second MCA album is "Liza Jane," which he wrote with Reed Nielsen. This exciting fun number finds Gill with a mad crush on Liza Jane, who never calls and never writes. This is one of the most successful of his songs about a fictional woman in his life. To date he has had musical "affairs" with a harem full of women, which include: "Liza Jane," "Lucy Dee," "Rita Ballou," and "Janny Lou" to name a few.

"If I Didn't Have You in My World" is a slow entry about devotion. On the country dance number "A Little Left Over," the singer is found watching the girls in cowboy hats at a bar on a Saturday night. The album concludes with the up-beat "Sparkle," which is one of the few really jubilant songs on this album. Written by the talented Jim Lauderdale, who is one of George Strait's favorite songwriters, the lyrics find Gill in an uncharacteristically giddy mood. Although *Pocket Full of Gold* isn't as cohesive as the *When I Call Your Name* album, it boasts several excellent songs, which show the Vince Gill legend in the making.

Vince observed at the time that his relationship with his wife, Janis, was usually the basis for his songwriting. In a roundabout way, all of the love songs were about her, as well as the ones that spoke of the frustrations of love. In that manner, Janis was very much a part of all of his music from this particular era of his career.

This was especially true on the song "Look at Us." "I started writing 'Look at Us,' " he explained in 1994 in the book *Country Hunks*, "and it changed depending on how Janis and I were getting along. At one point it was 'Look at us, we're blowin' it after all these years together.' And then we'd get along and it would be positive and then it would be sad again."

Vince admitted that he had borrowed some rock elements from other songs, and he had incorporated them into his music, to give his new album a more exciting sound. "I learn from a lot of people," he said in *Country Fever* in February 1993. "There's a difference between stealing and learning. 'Liza Jane' has a very similar feel to 'Lay Down Sally' [by Eric Clapton]. It's not exact, but it is the same kind of feel in the drums and the feel of it. Rodney Crowell's hit, 'Lovin' All Night,' has a similar feel to 'Lay Down Sally.' You could stand there and say that every country song with a straight rhythm guitar is a rip from the last forty or fifty years. I'm not ashamed to say where I've learned something. I'm not stupid enough to sit there and think, 'Well I thought of this all by myself.' It's another instance where my ego, hopefully, stays out of the way."

Speaking of rock 'n' roll guitars, in 1991 Vince was one of the guest players on the Dire Straits album *On Every Street*. He can be heard playing guitar throughout the LP. According to Dire Straits founder and lead singer, Mark Knopfler, he even offered Vince a spot in the rock group, but Gill declined. To say that Vince is standing in between rock 'n' roll and country is clearly an understatement. The fact of the matter is that he has always had one foot firmly planted in both styles of music.

The reviews for *Pocket Full of Gold* were unanimously glowing: "Again showing the enormity of his singing/songwriting/guitar-playing talents, Gill's *Pocket Full of Gold* shows his new-found success to be no fluke," claimed *Music City News*. "An exceptional tuneful and rhythmic record, *Pocket Full of Gold* tries to keep a positive attitude. In its plethora of 'he-she' songs. . . . Gill keeps his distance from standard country heartache themes, offering songs that celebrate success instead. . . . But no matter how easily it all goes down. . . . Gill has yet to write the kind of serious, poetic lyrics that would establish him as a complete artist," *Stereo Review* said prophetically.

In rapid succession, Vince scored four consecutive Top Ten hits from his second solo MCA album: "Pocket Full of Gold," "Liza Jane," "Look at Us," and "Take Your Memory with You." They peaked on the *Billboard Country* music charts successively at number seven, number seven, number four, and number two. The album *Pocket Full of Gold* went on to sell more than two million copies and was certified double platinum.

When the following year's array of awards ceremonies were held (presented in 1992 for 1991), Gill was back in the winner's circle for the accomplishments he had amassed in the past months. At the Country Music Association Awards, he was named 1991 Male Vocalist of the Year, and "When I Call Your Name" was chosen as their Song of the Year. To top it off, they selected "Restless," which Vince had recorded with Mark O'Connor, Steve Wariner, and Ricky Skaggs, the 1991 Vocal Event of the Year. Likewise, at the Grammy Awards on February 25, 1992, at New York City's Radio City Music Hall, Vince and Mark and Steve and

Ricky collected trophies when the Academy of Recorded Arts and Sciences gave them each a Grammy for the 1991 Best Country Vocal Collaboration, for "Restless." Accepting the Country Music Association Award, in the category of Vocal Event of the Year, for the song "Restless," he held up the trophy and announced, "This one's for the pickers out there!"

Gill later explained the evolution of the song "Restless," in *Modern Screen's Country* magazine (March 1992): "Actually it started out as a Carl Perkins rockabilly. It was fun to make. That kind of award is really for musicianship rather than vocal. I'll tell you, that Mark O'Connor is the best musician alive, bar none. He's the standard to which every musician working out there today has to judge himself."

At the same Country Music Association Awards held in Nashville, President George Bush and First Lady Barbara Bush were in the audience. When asked what goes through his head at these ceremonies, Vince told Mike Greenblatt of *Modern Screen's Country Music* magazine: "Nothing. I'm blank. I never plan anything to say, and I never will. To me, that's being a little presumptuous in thinking you'll win. I don't ever have those thoughts. I mean, I got up there and tried to zing the President with a one-liner. That's how goofy I am. But, it really is pretty terrifying. I have a hard time controlling my emotions. I do a lot better playing and singing 'cause that's what I'm familiar with."

Vince was now one of the biggest stars in country music. Along with Alan Jackson, Wynonna Judd, Reba McEntire, Garth Brooks, Brooks & Dunn, Mark Chesnutt, Colin Raye, and Tracy Lawrence, he represented the new sound of Nashville. In spite of this new-found notoriety, Gill remained pretty much unchanged in his outlook on life. He was still the same man who simply loved to make music and hang out with his golfing buddies. Now that he was becoming famous, he also had his share of mishaps to deal with. One of those unfortunate events came when he and his friend Rick Byrd were robbed at gunpoint at a golf course in the Bahamas.

As Vince detailed to the *Gavin Report* in early 1991: "I've got a whole bunch of golfing buddies. . . . It's a great release. I can go hang out with them and not have to talk charts and bullets and all that stuff. I hang out with a basketball coach named Rick Byrd—he's my best bud. . . . Rick got robbed with me in the Bahamas. I got held up at gunpoint while playing golf in the Bahamas. We played about five holes and these two guys came out of the middle of nowhere—one with a sawed-off shotgun and the other with a rifle. They took all our money, but we were grateful they didn't shoot us. . . . I was there at a basketball tournament. I go to the Bahamas for a basketball tournament—that's how weird I am."

Looking back on the incident with a sense of humor, Vince was later to joke in *Country Weekly* magazine (March 3, 1998): "I still get jumpy if somebody runs up on stage during a show."

Now that he was becoming a bona fide country superstar, Gill was quick to use his own personal time to give back to those less fortunate. One of the ways was to organize an annual charity basketball game, where he invited all of his singing buddies to come and play to raise money for local charities. Vince explained that this 1991 event was put together with his buddy Rick Byrd, who is the basketball coach at Belmont College in Nashville, Tennessee. When Rick told Vince that he needed to raise money for scholarships, the two of them came up with the idea of making it a celebrity event. As fellow basketball players, Gill invited industry buddies such as Rodney Crowell, Kathie Baillie, and Radney Foster.

More than 2,500 people attended, and a concert afterward sold out at the 1,200 seat auditorium at which it was held. The musicians not only had a ball on the court, but they also raised the necessary funds.

Now that he had achieved a great deal of success in the country music realm, Vince began to ponder the question of whether fame was all that it was cracked up to be. According to him, during this time he was having a lot of fun with it. His life was also going through a lot of changes as his popularity grew.

As mentioned earlier, Vince became more and more successful as, at the same time, things had begun to slow down for his wife, Janis, and Sweethearts of the Rodeo. The tables had turned, and people began to speculate if she felt any resentment toward him. "I don't think so," he said to *Modern Screen's Country* magazine for their Fall 1991 issue: "I think for the majority of the time, which is what really matters, we've been each other's support system. We've been married for eleven years. So we've hung on together through a lot of stuff. I truly don't feel our careers will have that much of an impact on our marriage. She's writing now for their next album."

As 1991 was winding toward a close, Vince Gill was preparing for even greater career success in the new year. He found himself more in demand than ever before. He was on the threshold of becoming one of the most famous and successful singers that Nashville had ever produced. And, it was only the beginning.

SIX

I STILL BELIEVE IN YOU

While Vince was racking up awards during the first two years of the 1990s, the whole realm of country music was changing in a significant way that would alter the way record buyers would look at the genre forever. It was in 1991 when *Billboard* magazine switched its method of tallying album sales of every genre, and it was discovered that country artists such as Garth Brooks were actually selling more copies of their albums than had been reported previously. This new method of tallying sales using the bar-coding on CDs and cassettes actually counted sales at the cash registers. It is known as Soundscan. Because of it, suddenly country music invaded the pop album charts. With this development, Brooks's 1991 release *Ropin' the Wind* became the first album ever to enter the *Billboard* pop album chart at number one. Likewise, Vince Gill was now sharing chart space beside the likes of Metallica and M. C. Hammer.

When 1991 ended, Vince's *Pocket Full of Gold* was on the *Billboard* 200 Top Albums chart at number forty, wedged somewhere in between Prince's *Diamonds & Pearls* and Van Halen's *For Unlawful Carnal Knowledge*. Now country music was competing in the big leagues and selling more copies of each album than ever before in its genre. It was the era of country music's big explosion and expansion, and Vince Gill was part of the excitement as well as being part of the reason for it. In addition, the increased record sales meant the promotion of a fresh batch of music stars who could sell out concert halls, theaters, and auditoriums. Vince was to benefit greatly from this new development as well by becoming a top draw on the concert circuit.

Looking ahead, *People* magazine asked Gill for his New Year's resolutions for 1992, and he replied, "I don't know if I ever made any! I wish I could be a little more organized and not drive people crazy. I just kind of run when the sun comes up and do what I wanna do. I don't play as good as I should." That was his opinion. Clearly he was in the eye of the storm, and he couldn't see the winning streak that was looming ahead for him.

In 1992 Vince released his classic *I Still Believe in You,* and it was to become the biggest selling album of his career to date. It was a ten-cut LP made up almost entirely of insightful ballads. The exceptions were a fun country rock number, "One More Last Chance," and the light-hearted and fast-paced "Pretty Words" was in the middle just for good measure. These two songs served to shift gears in between such heartfelt ballads as "No Future in the Past," "I Still Believe in You," and the effervescent "Don't Let Our Love Start Slippin' Away." This record was a sure-fire hits package from this musically talented Oklahoma boy.

Furthermore, the album's packaging and artwork brilliantly played up the hunk look of Vince's physique and chiseled handsome face. He was very trim and in shape during this period, and photographer Victoria Pearson Cameron captured him at his most 1990s *GQ* magazine model-like self. Well-groomed, and standing smart in sharp designer suits and jackets, the six-foot-three-inch-tall Gill had a great look. The CD package featured seven photos in black-and-white and color which played up the image makeover, taking him from good-guy guitar player of next door to sexy leading man. The videos that he starred in from this album were also among his best, capitalizing on his sex appeal. There was a huge focus on country music that year on television, on the radio, and on magazine covers. And, Vince Gill was in the middle of all this excitement.

The reviews for *I Still Believe in You* were absolutely glowing: "Gill easily breaks enough new ground here to avoid merely lapsing into old formula . . . a real standout song is 'Under These Conditions,' co-written with Max D. Barnes. . . . On a slow, tasty ballad such as this, Gill's high, sweet tenor voice soars far above Nashville's flooded sea of cowboy hats," said *Country America* magazine. "Writing or co-writing every song included, Gill seems to be growing in leaps and bounds as a tunesmith with each outing . . . . Album has romantic 'Nothing Like a Woman' to hilarious 'One More Last Chance'—borderline cheating 'Under These Conditions.' . . . the singer paints vivid portraits of love in various stages, delivered with the most heavenly voice imaginable," proclaimed *Music City News*. And, David Zimmerman (*USA Today*) decided: "Gill, thirty-five, is already off to a fast start. The title song from the new album, *I Still Believe in You* (*** 1/2), went to number one Monday in *Billboard*. It's the first sampling of his best album ever, one that's heavy on ballads and perfectly constructed around his heartbreak vocals and bluegrass-honed proficiency on electric piano."

In July 1992, the first single off the new album, "I Still Believe in You," sailed into the Top Forty of *Billboard* magazine's Hot Country Singles chart, and it didn't stop until it went all the way to number one. It became Gill's first chart-topping hit, followed in rapid succession by "Don't Let Our Love Keep Slippin' Away," which became his second number-one hit of 1992. Finally, Vince Gill was on the winning streak he had so long dreamed of attaining.

According to Vince, the song "I Still Believe in You" was definitely one that was written about his relationship with Janis. He had come home from a long road tour to Nashville for only twenty-four hours, and he chose to spend it working with one of his songwriting partners. As he told *Country Fever* (February 1993): "We were trying to squeeze about two months of catching up into twenty-four hours and it just didn't work. . . . It was a real frustrating time, and I almost canceled the songwriting date. But I went on and left." Vince explains, "I had a writing date with John Jarvis. . . . But before I went over there, I had a big fight with Janis. A major-leave big fight. One of the ugliest we've ever had. And I don't remember what it was all about. It's all words. Never physical. . . . I got over there with John and was kind of shell-shocked by the fight and what it was all about and he says, 'What's up?' and I said, 'Man, it seems like just everybody wants a piece of my time.' And that was basically how it got going."

Jarvis is the one who took Vince's words and drew out the rest of the story. "His ears perked up and he said, 'That's a good start.' He played a tune and I poured out the words. It was really neat because it wound up being a nice apology," Gill said in *TV Guide* in the fall of 1993.

Now that he was producing back-to-back number-one singles, Vince found that, suddenly, he was very much in demand. Still, he insisted on taking as much time as he needed on each album. "I think that it's hard to be machinelike," he claimed in *Country Fever* (March 1993). "It's just worked out that that's how long it's taken between records. I don't know if they'd like them any sooner, but they're doin' well and selling lots of records, so I don't see any point in shutting off the pipeline."

The only cut on *I Still Believe in You* written by Vince alone was "Tryin' to Get Over You." The rest of them were co-written with others. According to him, he enjoyed the camaraderie, and he appreciated having another person's perspective to draw upon. He didn't want every song he created to be based on his own personal life; he wanted to have more universal themes to sing about.

In addition to his growing success in Nashville, and through-out the country, Vince was also being acknowledged for his unselfish nature. Meanwhile that year, he was nominated for eight TNN/*Music City News* Country Awards. When the trophies were handed out on June 8, 1992, he won for Best Instrumental-ist of the Year. That night he dedicated his award to drummer Lar-rie Londin who was hospitalized after suffering a heart attack.

That same month in 1992, simultaneously with Nashville's annual country star festival, Fan Fair, Vince won a TNN/*Music City News* Award, this time around as Best Instrumentalist. He was most flattered by this honor. According to him, he started as a guitar player, so this was an especially meaningful trophy to add to his collection.

Now riding high, Gill took time to share his voice and his musi-cianship on albums by others as well. He was heard throughout the album *Sisters* by Sweethearts of the Rodeo, both as a musician and as a background singer. That particular release was produced by Steve Buckingham and singer/songwriter Wendy Waldman.

The album included the highly personal song "Sisters (Best of Friends)," and a number about Vince: "Man of My Dreams." In the lyrics of that song, Janis Gill sings that the man of her dreams doesn't pick up his clothes, never sends her flowers, and stares at the TV endlessly. On the plus side, she sings that he can sure sing and play guitar, and that he has won her heart.

He was also one of the country and rock singers to appear on the *Honeymoon in Vegas* (1992) soundtrack. The big-screen fare starred Nicolas Cage, Sarah Jessica Parker, and James Caan. It was about a man (Cage) who promises his mother on her deathbed never to marry. This vow causes complications when he and Parker venture to Las Vegas to tie the knot, and he again gets cold feet. When Caan beats Cage at poker, Cage must allow his fiancée to have a date with him. Suddenly, the reluctant bridegroom is put on the defensive.

The album and the film both had an Elvis Presley theme to them. In the comedy, there was a group of parachuting Elvis impersonators, and on the soundtrack, several singing stars provided their personal interpretations of classic Presley songs. The album itself is quite a treat, with or without having seen the accompanying film. On the disc, Billy Joel delivers a slammin' "All Shook Up," Ricky Van Shelton sings a snapping "Wear My Ring Around Your Neck," and Dwight Yoakam zings in a moody "Suspicious Minds." Amy Grant turns "Love Me Tender" into a romantic ballad, Willie Nelson gets mellow with "Blue Hawaii," and Bono turns "Can't Help Falling in Love" into lounge lizard crooning. In the middle of this comes Vince Gill's rockabilly version of "That's All Right," which had been among Elvis Presley's first professional recordings for Sun Records in the 1950s.

Vince was also one of the guest performers to be heard on country legend George Jones's 1992 album *Walls Can Fall* (MCA Records). Along with Mark Chesnutt, Garth Brooks, Travis Tritt, Joe Diffie, Alan Jackson, Pam Tillis, T. Graham Brown, Patty Loveless, and Clint Black, Gill was among the guest stars making a cameo vocal appearance on the song "I Don't Need Your Rockin' Chair." With a little help from his younger friends, George Jones hit number thirty-four on the charts with this entry about longevity and determination—two attributes which Jones's own career has been built upon.

Speaking of Gill, George Jones claimed in *TV Guide* (October 1, 1994): "Vince has got to be the nicest person I have ever met, both in and out of the music business. A fine musician and a great artist, he brings back the sound of country music like it used to be in the early days."

When Reba McEntire was recording her 1992 album, *It's Your Call* (MCA Records), she asked Vince to sing a duet with her on it. He gladly obliged, and the resulting song, "The Heart Won't Lie," became a huge 1993 number-one hit for the duo when it was released as a single. This gave Gill three number-one songs in a row! There was no stopping him now.

The video that was shot to accompany "The Heart Won't Lie" made Vince and Reba look like bona fide movie stars. Ever since she played a costarring role in the monster movie *Tremors* (1990), she had been actively advancing her career by becoming a full-fledged screen actress. Reba's desire to get involved in acting paid off on this effective mini-movie.

During this productive period, one magazine article after another proclaimed that Vince was the Nashville hunk to watch. Gill laughed at the notion. When it came time to shoot his new video, he wanted to poke fun at his growing hunk status. When McEntire submitted the original shooting script for the video of "The Heart Won't Lie," it called for Vince and Reba to be outfitted as enlisted officers, with Gill portraying a Marine. Reba wanted it to look like Richard Gere and Debra Winger in the film *An Officer and a Gentleman* (1982). According to Vince, as reported in the book *Country Hunks* (1994), he suggested a mocking variation in which he "played Gomer Pyle instead of Richard Gere! Reba was gonna be LouAnn Poovey, but it wouldn't work out. They [the producers] wouldn't go for my idea of Gomer and LouAnn as Marines."

Happily, Reba's version won out. The resulting video is very moving and sets off the hit song beautifully. With that, it became fair game to ask whether Vince was intending to head into movies.

He certainly has the good looks, and the pleasant easy-going manner that is appealing on screen.

Also in 1992, MCA released Vince's first compilation of his videos. Under the title *I Still Believe in You*, this home video includes six of his most popular songs brought to life. The entries on this audio/visual album are "When I Call Your Name," "Never Knew Lonely," "Pocket Full of Gold," "Liza Jane," "Look at Us," and "I Still Believe in You."

As evidenced in this package, Vince's videos are generally moody pieces where he is depicted singing his songs simply with unusual backdrops or atmospheric locations for support. He doesn't give them elaborate plots or choreography like Reba McEntire or Brooks & Dunn. His first one, "When I Call Your Name," is very simple and sepia-toned, with Gill seen crooning in interesting hallways or while gazing out of the window of a Southern mansion. Also sepia-toned, the "Never Knew Lonely" video finds Vince driving a 1950s automobile on a desolate road and sitting in a lonely-looking motel room.

The "Pocket Full of Gold" video casts Vince as a barroom singer at a roadside honky-tonk, and he lets professional actors portray the cheating characters in the plot of the song. The video of "Liza Jane" begins with Vince in a varsity letter jacket, standing outdoors at a drive-in movie, explaining to the camera how the rain ruined all of their flashy filming plans. What ensues instead is an impromptu concert at the concession stand of the drive-in. Finally, toward the end of the song, the rain clears enough to shoot outdoors, where Gill and the cast are seen dancing with umbrellas and fireworks in the wet weather.

The sentimental "Look at Us" gets a nostalgic video treatment, made entirely of old home movies, incorporated with new footage of Vince and Janis kissing and cuddling. The video concludes with "I Still Believe in You," another atmospheric piece showing off a handsome and suited Mr. Gill, singing the song in a lovely and deserted concert hall. Although light on plot, the videos served up substantial amounts of an appealing Gill in closeups.

Still, Vince was the first to scoff at the notion that he was regarded as a heartthrob, a hunk, or a pinup guy.

As to his sudden streak of success, he claimed to be amazed. In his own mind, he was just playing the same four chords he had always sung. Oh, but what a great four chords he sang in, so expressive, so wonderful to listen to on disc or in concert. Vince's personal modesty was, and still is, part of his enduring appeal. Granted, it wasn't just the timbre or the technical sound of his voice, but it was the way he expressed himself. The lyrics he wrote were about heartfelt themes that a very wide audience could appreciate. It didn't matter whether his new-found audience was connecting with his sensitive and insightful side (like on the song "Look at Us"), or his playful mode (as on the tune "Rita Ballou"), his career was gaining great momentum.

One of the reasons for the wide audience acceptance of Vince's music was that it was just plain good music. Right from the very start he was appealing to record buyers who were country fans, and by other startled music fans who never thought they would find themselves even listening to what used to be called country-western music.

As he was now beginning to read about himself in magazines and hear himself on the radio, he appeared to have a good handle on the whole dynamic of fame. Said Vince in the March 1993 issue of *Modern Screen's Country* magazine. "The one thing I've realized, from the time I was in the group Pure Prairie League right up until today, is that this fame stuff is fleeting. . . . When I first came to Nashville, everybody was saying how, because of the fact that I was an instrumentalist, a songwriter, and a vocalist, I'd be such a huge star. Well, it never happened for the longest time, and nobody could understand why. *That's* pressure. Now, I'm relieved. I don't feel I have to top this or that. I don't feel I have to keep doing things better and better. I know in my heart that if I continue to just do the best work I know how, everything's going to fall where it falls."

During this period of his rise to fame, both Vince and Janis admitted that their marriage had passed through some rocky phases. On the subject of their union, Janis told *People* magazine (June 10, 1991): "Our child probably has been the cement at times when things got tough and when maybe it might have been easier to say, 'I've had it.'"

Interestingly, in all of their years together, with both of their careers as singers and as songwriters, Vince and Janis had never yet written a song as a team. According to Vince in the same article, "We probably will, but it's tough enough. We don't need to be arguing about what should rhyme with what." However, it would not happen for a few more years.

At the time, Rodney Crowell and Rosanne Cash had split up, and she took her frustrations over the demise of her marriage and turned them into songs for her album *The Wheel* (1993). Commenting at the time about it in *Modern Screen's Country* magazine, Vince said, "Well, her and Rodney wear their relationship on their sleeve. We're [Vince and Janis] not quite so public about it. Hey, we're married, y'know. There's good days and bad days and you can only hope the good outnumber the bad. We've lasted a long time."

It was Janis who pointed out in *People*: "We are opposites in many, many ways. I listen to classical music, and he listens to bluegrass. He plays golf, and I sew. He's the most organized person you've ever seen, and I have to have it spotless or I can't be normal. He's laid back, and I'm stressed out. He's so relaxed, he can slide down in a chair, but I always have to be doing something."

Explaining how he and Janis juggled raising their daughter, Gill had told *Modern Screen's Country* magazine in the fall of 1991: "We have a full time governess who lives with us. Plus, Jenny's days are filled with school. She's a busy kid and she's adjusted quite well to all of this. She comes out on tours with us in the summer to all the state fairs. She's real normal. She'd rather watch Nickelodeon than mom or dad on TV. We're best buddies, and that's really neat. I go to as many of her ball games as I can."

"I always tell her when I lay down at night that when I'm not here with her, to feel her heart, and I'm inside there," he reported in *People* (June 10, 1991). "I bring her things from the road, out-fits, jewelry. My guilt feelings take over, and I come home and shower her with presents. . . . She handles it better than we do."

Now that his life was so hectic, with constant touring and personal appearances, Vince was well aware that his career was taking a good deal of time away from his family. As he said to *Modern Screen's Country* in 1991: "I'm gonna look back in ten years and probably feel pretty crappy for all the time spent away from her."

According to Gill, having both of her parents in show business didn't affect Jenny at all: "The bottom line for me is that I honestly believe that she understands what I do and why I'm not home a lot. I'd know if she wasn't adjusting or handling it well. My daughter and I are really close in a most remarkable way," he said to the same publication the following year.

Watching his daughter suddenly begin to grow up that year was something that totally amazed him. "Jenny turned ten in May," he said in 1993 in *Country Fever*. "Seems like she's been seventeen. I've been tellin' everybody when she gets [to be] thirteen, I'm comin' off the road till she gets into college. That's the deal. Boys can come—if they can whip me, they can take her out. It's really fun to watch her grow up."

Vince's parents had since separated, and they lived in different states. His father was in Columbus, Ohio, and his mother was in Oklahoma City, Oklahoma. Speaking of his dad, Vince said at the time, "He's a Federal Appellate Court Judge. He hears appeals for the social security system. People who have had their benefits denied. So he's not a real popular guy. Doesn't get to hear a lot of good stuff. Mom, my sister, and my brother are in Oklahoma City. Everybody's doing good. Grandma's in Kansas. Aunts and uncles in Kansas. Everybody's doing good." Although Janis's group, Sweethearts of the Rodeo, was still active on the concert circuit, Vince and his wife were almost never seen on the same stage, let alone in the same town. According to Gill, "We're going to do one date this year together. We did one date last year. It was great. It was a date. We went out and ate corn dogs together."

In spite of the fact that he was now a huge singing star, Vince continued to make time to go into the recording studio to appear on other people's albums. He was simply so in love with the process of making good music that he never minded if he was the star, the costar, or a star in the background. He never objected to taking direction in the studio either. "Well, there's nothing wrong with that," he explained for the February 1993 edition of *Country Fever* magazine. "That's part of your job when working for somebody else. Sometimes that's what is called for. Sometimes people don't want your opinion, and that's fine. . . . If they ask you what you think, you tell 'em and offer whatever they want to hear. There are no rules." He was also, reportedly, among the highest paid background singers in Nashville. "Highest paid?" Vince joked at the notion. "I just work for [musician's union] scale. I just work for the same price everybody else does."

Nonetheless, the biggest career milestone for Vince Gill in 1992 was his being asked to join the prestigious Grand Ole Opry as an active member. This distinguished roster also included Dolly Parton, Ricky Skaggs, Randy Travis, George Jones, Alan Jackson, Buck Owens, Merle Haggard, and an ever-growing list of country music's best and brightest stars.

Finally, after three albums for MCA Records, Vince Gill's career was red hot. He had become one of the most popular and most in-demand singers in Nashville. Now that he had arrived professionally, the challenge was to maintain the momentum his career was experiencing and continue to stretch out musically.

SEVEN

I CAN'T TELL YOU WHY

As 1993 began, Vince Gill's song "Don't Let Our Love Start Slippin' Away" was still high on the music charts. The easy-going Oklahoma singer, now thirty-five, had assuredly staked out a unique niche for himself in contemporary country music. It was officially a whole new regime for Nashville: new acts, new blood, a new generation of record buyers, and a new batch of stars to bring concertgoers to the box-office, and Vince was maximizing his success in a multimedia way.

To appropriately borrow a term from the Eagles: It was as though a new batch of *desperados* had ridden into town, and taken it over. As though casting a western movie from classic Hollywood, everyone had their distinctive roles. Garth Brooks had established himself as the wild country rocker. Alan Jackson was the smooth Southern crooner. Clint Black was the gentlemanly Texan. Travis Tritt was the motorcycle-riding Southern country rocker. Dwight Yoakam was playing the aloof traditionalist in skin-tight jeans. Brooks & Dunn were the country troubadours in the mode of Simon & Garfunkel. George Strait was the quintessential Texan rodeo singer. Billy Ray Cyrus was the year's achy breaky new hunk on the block. And then there was Vince Gill: the suburban country balladeer and weekend golfer.

It seemed that, by now, Vince was amassing awards and accolades by the truckload. His music represented a breath of fresh air in a town full of cowboy wannabes and straw-chewing stereotypes. Gill was a totally 1990s ballad singer whose appeal stretched much wider than the stylistic constraints of country, bluegrass, or the new traditionalist sound that was sweeping the industry.

On February 24, 1993, the annual Grammy Awards were held in Los Angeles at the Shrine Auditorium. That evening, Vince Gill was nominated for two of the top awards. In the category of Best Country Vocal Performance, Male, his album *I Still Believe in You* was up against Garth Brooks's album *The Chase*, Billy Ray Cyrus's single "Achy Breaky Heart," Randy Travis's single "Better Class of Losers," and Travis Tritt's single "Lord Have Mercy on the Working Man."

In the songwriter's category of Best Country Song, Vince and John Barlow Jarvis's composition "I Still Believe in You" was competing with "Achy Breaky Heart" (Don Von Tress songwriter, Billy Ray Cyrus singer), "I Feel Lucky" (Mary Chapin Carpenter and Don Schlitz songwriters, Mary Chapin Carpenter singer), "She Is His Only Need" (Dave Loggins songwriter, Wynonna Judd singer), and "The Greatest Man I Never Knew" (Richard Leigh and Layng Martine Jr. songwriters, Reba McEntire singer).

Vince didn't just win one of the coveted awards—he won both of them—much to his surprise. In an era where Garth Brooks seemed to be grabbing every conceivable prize he was nominated for, Gill proved worthy competition! According to Vince in *Modern Screen's Country* magazine (March 1992): "Each award show is different. I won at the Grammys and he [Garth Brooks] didn't, although everybody thought he would. And I'd hate to think that he was the only competition. That's not fair to George Strait, Alan Jackson, and Clint Black. In fact, I really thought Alan was going to do well, and he didn't. But I was very pleased. To be honored as a songwriter is just the best."

Gill also got himself into a bit of controversy on the televised awards shows. In a charity climate which called for performers to wear a red ribbon to show support for AIDS awareness, yellow ribbons for . . . , and so forth, he refused to wear any color of ribbon. At first, he took a lot of heat in the press for being unsympathetic toward charitable causes. According to him, however, he simply wasn't going to kowtow to anyone, or to show favoritism for any one cause by turning his back on another.

————————

In early 1993 Vince Gill was one of the celebrities in Palm Springs, California, for the Bob Hope Desert Classic Golf Tournament, an annual charity event. Vince was invited as one of the performers at the banquet, which is an all-star event. The reason that Vince was included to attend this event, which is truly part of the bastion of old guard Hollywood and show business, is due to promoter/producer Pete Bennett. A show business legend unto himself, Bennett has worked as a record promoter for many big names in show business from Nat King Cole and Frank Sinatra, to the Beatles and the Rolling Stones. Pete had heard Vince's music and was a big fan of his.

"Who is this guy, Vince Gill?" Bob Hope asked Pete Bennett when the country singer's name was brought up for the tournament. "Maybe you haven't heard of him yet, Mr. Hope," Pete said to the legendary comedian, "but he is one of the biggest up-and-coming performers in country music. Forget-about-it, he's fantastic, you're gonna love him."

With that, as Bennett told this author in 1998, Hope agreed to add him to the list of performers. The night of Vince's performance, the audience was mainly in the age range of sixty-five on upward. According to Bennett, at first the applause was only modest. Then, Vince's winning personality captivated the audience. The following year Bob Hope said to Pete, "Can you get that Vince Gill guy, I kinda liked him." Even Bob Hope, in his nineties, had become a Vince Gill fan.

———•◦◦•◦◦•———

Although there was one glorious triumph after another for Vince in 1993, this time was not without its own share of sadness and grief. It was the year that Vince's older brother Bob died. Vince was deeply hurt, and he channeled his grief in his public statements and ultimately in his music.

In the spring of 1993, Vince Gill was one of the country music singing stars who were inducted into Nashville's Starwalk attraction at Opryland, USA. In addition to Vince, Bill Monroe, Emmylou Harris, and songwriters Don Henry and John Barlow Jarvis were also inducted. At the ceremony, Vince not only carved his handprints into the cement, but he also stuck a few golf tees into the wet concrete as well. According to Gill, his late brother had given him golf tees the past Christmas. To make his sibling a part of the ceremony, Vince stuck several tees in the concrete in remembrance.

When the TNN/*Music City News* Awards were handed out, Vince took four of the top prizes: 1993 Album of the Year for *I Still Believe in You*, 1993 Single of the Year for "I Still Believe in You," Instrumentalist of the Year, and the 1993 Minnie Pearl Award for Humanitarianism in raising money for charity. Accepting the honor with tears in his eyes, Vince said sincerely, "I'm truly speechless. . . . I figured I had to do this for thirty or forty years."

When he was presented with the award for the song "I Still Believe in You," Vince stood up before the audience filled with his peers and started talking about his wife, Janis, who was sitting in the audience that night. As reported in *Star,* Gill said, "There is no better inspiration than my wife. She's done this for a long time. She's a good songwriter, too. So, honey, I'm going to give this to you." To the audience he announced, "We've been apart for as many as 200 days a year. I hardly ever saw Janis. Now we're going to stay home more, because our marriage is more important than even this wonderful award. . . . My career sometimes takes me away from Janis and my baby for weeks at a time. There are inspirations for songs. I have no better one than my wife, so I'm giving this award to her. She has never gotten awards or anything, but she's a good songwriter, too. So, honey, I want to give this to you."

After her husband gave her the award, Janis Gill said in the *Star:* "I was sure he was going to acknowledge a particular writer who'd influenced him when he was young. He's always doing that, putting the focus on somebody else. I could not believe he talked about me. It totally blew me away."

As the year progressed, it seemed like a clean sweep for singing star Gill. At the Country Music Association Awards, Vince took home a variety of trophies: the 1993 Album of the Year for *I Still Believe in You,* the 1993 Song of the Year for "I Still Believe in You," the 1993 Male Vocalist of the Year, and the 1993 Vocal Event of the Year for "I Don't Need Your Rockin' Chair" by George Jones with Vince Gill, Mark Chesnutt, Garth Brooks, Travis Tritt, Joe Diffie, Alan Jackson, Pam Tillis, T. Graham Brown, Patty Loveless, and Clint Black. As if that wasn't sufficient, Gill was also named the Country Music Association's 1993 Entertainer of the Year!

Later, when he was asked if winning the Entertainer of the Year Award from the CMA made a career difference, Vince told *Country Fever* magazine in mid-1994: "The money is a little better, and a few more people are showing up. I don't make a big deal out of it, just because that's my makeup. I wouldn't want the people at the CMA and those who have bestowed that honor upon me to think I don't care about it. People were offended when I made a crack that a 'hole-in-one' [on the golf course] was a lot more exciting. . . . I was just joking. . . . Winning that award is the neatest thing. It's a great validation of what I've been doing, but it doesn't change me."

At the Academy of Country Music Awards in 1993, Gill was selected the Top Male Vocalist of the Year, and he and Jim Jarvis won the Song of the Year trophy for "I Still Believe in You." Accepting the prize, Vince dedicated it to the memory of his brother.

Although sad about the passing of his beloved brother Bob, Gill still retained his sense of humor at the ceremony. Speaking about the nine-year gap between winning the 1984 Best New Artist Award from the Academy of Country Music, and the 1993 Male Vocalist Award, Vince joked that he now held the record for the longest span between winning Best New Artist and Best Male Vocalist in the history of the Academy of Country Music. It was Gill himself who quipped that although his music hadn't improved, his golf game sure had!

In addition to all of these honors, when BMI music publishing handed out their annual songwriter's awards, they declared three of Vince's recordings to be among their tally of 1993 Most Performed Songs. The honors that year went to "I Still Believe in You," "Don't Let Our Love Start Slippin' Away," and "Take Your Memory with You."

As for Gill's golf game, it had been a banner year for that as well. At the Pro Am Tournament at the Phoenix Open in Scottsdale,

Arizona, Vince hit a hole-in-one. People began to wonder if he was going to quit country for a career on the links. Tackling that issue in *Country Fever* magazine (February 1993), Vince proclaimed: "No. I could not make it on the pro tour. . . . I couldn't beat all the guys in Nashville, and I gotta beat all the guys in Nashville before I can go beat all the guys on the tour. I know better. . . . Maybe when I was eighteen, if I had gone to college and played golf and hit 500 balls a day for several years and done all the things that you have to do [to] get to that level, then maybe, yeah, I could go out there and play with them."

In mid-1993, the big debate in the music business concerned the resale of compact discs in retail stores. Several record companies threatened certain retail chain stores—Wherehouse among them—with cancellation of their products in their stores for selling "used" discs alongside new discs. It was the greed topic of the year, and everyone seemed to be getting into the act. Vince managed to stay out of the fray, until he was cornered by the *Los Angeles Times* that fall at a music industry function. When pressured to state his opinion, he decreed diplomatically, "It's tough to take sides, because both sides are totally valid arguments. I can see the record industry point of view, because songwriters deserve royalties. But if somebody buys their CD, they've already been paid once. So both sides make sense."

As an avid music-maker Vince was paying close attention to what was going on in the music scene. To stay current with what was happening on the music charts, Gill admitted that his car radio is often his listening room and that he loves to hear a wide variety of music, not just country. "I like to listen to Bonnie Raitt as much, or more, than anybody," he told *Country Fever* magazine that year. "I think she's the greatest singer. Any kind of music. And she's a good friend, and I'm really proud that she's doing so well. She's deserved it for twenty years. I like the new band Little Village. I listen a little bit to everything. . . . I like anything good."

During 1993, Vince Gill made some of the most eclectic music of his career. His releases included rock 'n' roll, country swing, 1970s California pop, and Christmas music. In the rock 'n' roll realm, Vince was heard with the legendary rock band Little Feat on the soundtrack album to the 1993 drama *Indecent Proposal*. The film, which starred Demi Moore, Woody Harrelson, and Robert Redford, was set in Las Vegas—just like *Honeymoon in Vegas*. The album is an effectively moody entry featuring several country and rock stars singing slow and somber versions of famous rock songs, perfect for setting the scene for the weighty emotional turmoil that takes place in the plot of the movie.

The *Indecent Proposal* soundtrack album includes such gems as the Pretenders singing "I'm Not in Love," Bryan Ferry crooning "Will You Love Me Tomorrow," and Sheena Easton getting jazzy on Hoagy Carmichael's classic, "The Nearness of You." Original contributions included Seal's moody "Out of the Window" and Lisa Stansfield's sultry "In All the Right Places." It was a diverse but very contemporary group to be heard in the company of, and Vince's song was one of the album's highlights. Singing the Allen Toussaint composition "What Do You Want the Girl to Do?" Gill performed with rock's Little Feat. Not an ounce of country is heard on this perfect medium tempo rocker. It was the song that had opened Bonnie Raitt's *Home Plate* album in 1975, and Vince did a great interpretation of this ballad about the frustrations of love.

When Ray Benson, the leader of the country swing band Asleep at the Wheel, decided to pay tribute to the legendary Bob Wills & His Texas Playboys, he pulled out all of the stops. The 1993 album, *Tribute to Bob Wills* by Asleep at the Wheel and, literally, a Who's Who of Nashville, was an incredible gem. In real life, Bob Wills was known for his crying out "haw" or "ye haw" in the middle of a song, or verbally directing a soloist to "come on in" for a solo during a number. Mimicking the Wills style of recording live in the studio, Benson presided masterfully over an all-star roster of guests including George Strait, Dolly Parton, Chet Atkins, Marty Stuart, Suzy Bogguss, Lyle Lovett, Garth Brooks, Huey Lewis, Willie Nelson, Merle Haggard, and Vince Gill.

The opening song is "Red Wing," an instrumental number featuring Vince on electric guitar, Johnny Gimble on fiddle, Marty Stuart on electric mandolin, Chet Atkins on gut string guitar, and Lucky Oceans on the Hawaiian steel guitar. Gill is also heard as the lead singer on the Appalachian sounding "Yearning (Just for You)."

According to Ray Benson in the liner notes of the Liberty album, "I first heard Merle Haggard do it on Bob Wills & His Texas Playboys' *For the Last Time* album. When I called up Vince to ask him what song he wanted to do, he asked about this one. He, too, had heard it on the same legendary album and wanted to sing it. We recorded it during the day of his show at the Austin Rodeo. Vince, besides being an amazing singer and guitarist, is a downright nice guy—until he gets a basketball in his hands."

This album represents country music at its most 1940s/1950s Grand Ole Opry peak. Unlike the big band swing sound of Glenn Miller and Tommy Dorsey, which 1990s bands such as Cherry Poppin' Daddies and the Brian Setzer Orchestra have revived,

Texas swing is one part hillbilly, one part swing, one part Texas rodeo, and a lot of fiddle playing. This is one excellent album, and Vince sounds great on it.

The height of success that the 1993 album *Common Thread: The Songs of the Eagles* achieved was phenomenal. With a singing lineup that was the cream of 1990s Nashville, this tribute album has stood brilliantly on its own as one of the best albums of this sort ever recorded. The individual performers each took their own country stylings and presented their interpretation of their favorite Eagles song. Travis Tritt's rocking "Take It Easy," Tanya Tucker ripping into "Already Gone," Brooks & Dunn's searing "Best of My Love," and John Anderson's snappy "Heartache Tonight" gave the album life and sizzle. Presenting the ballad side of things, Suzy Bogguss's "Take It to the Limit," Trisha Yearwood's "New Kid in Town," and Vince Gill's "I Can't Tell You Why" gave it a lot of heart.

Besides being a wonderfully inspired offering, *Common Thread: The Songs of the Eagles* went on to become a huge success, hitting number one on the Country Albums chart and number three on the *Billboard* 200 Albums chart. It sold more than four million copies and is one of the most successful all-star tribute albums ever recorded. It was a great project for Vince to have been featured on, and he sounded most impressive on it.

Meanwhile, the faltering Sweethearts of the Rodeo switched recording companies from Columbia to a smaller label, Sugar Hill. In 1993, the group released *Rodeo Waltz*, which was produced by Janis Gill. Vince made a guest appearance on the album, and it is most notable for including his composition, "Jenny Dreamed of Trains," which was written about their daughter. Unfortunately, while Vince's career was soaring from one height to another, Janis's was floundering further and further away from the cutting edge of what was happening in contemporary country music. None of the songs on this album even cracked *Billboard* magazine's Country Top Forty chart.

On the other hand, throughout 1993 Vince was releasing one hit single after another. He followed up his number-one duet with Reba McEntire with "No Future in the Past," which peaked at number three. In the summer of 1993 came the up-tempo "One More Last Chance," which sailed straight up the charts and didn't stop until it, too, reached number one. The amusing video that accompanied it lampooned his love of the game of golf. In one of the sequences, Vince is seen driving his golf cart right into a pond.

Late in 1993, Vince released two separate Christmas holiday projects. At Target department stores throughout the country, he could be heard with Trisha Yearwood on a special promotional single marketed for children called "Another Angel Gets Its Wings."

That same season, Vince released his first full album of Christmas music, entitled *Let There Be Peace on Earth*. It was produced by Tony Brown. Instead of making it an album of country-tinged holiday tunes, Gill chose instead to go the middle-of-the-road route, with full orchestra and a background chorus supporting him. This was quite different than what his contemporaries were recording on their holiday offerings. For instance, when Alan Jackson did his debut Christmas album, *Honky Tonk Christmas* (Arista Records, 1993), he went all out to make it country sounding, including such songs as "Santa's Gonna Come in a Pickup Truck" and "Please Daddy (Don't Get Drunk This Christmas)."

Vince's album was styled similar to recordings of such performers as Johnny Mathis, Tony Bennett, and Mel Torme. These artists were all famous popular/jazz singers and recording artists of the 1950s and early 1960s, and their romantic, highly orchestrated albums became the traditional pop soundtracks of the era. Gill's fans immediately responded favorably, making the release a million-selling, platinum-certified smash. Only the instrumental song "Santa Claus Is Coming to Town" has a fast-paced tone, featuring the star's most tasteful guitar picking on it. In fact it has such a swing tone that it could nearly qualify as a Bob Wills & His Texas Playboys arrangement of that holiday classic. When the album was released that Christmas, it sailed up the *Billboard* magazine Top 200 Albums chart to number fourteen in December and to number three on that magazine's Country Albums chart.

One of the most memorable cuts on this Christmas album was "Let There Be Peace on Earth," which featured a very special guest artist: eleven-year-old Jenny Gill, making her recording debut. She had performed the song previously for a school program. For Gill, working with his daughter on this number for his album was a very special moment.

The one Gill original composition that appears on this album, the sad song "It Won't Be the Same This Year," Vince dedicated to his late brother, Bob. On the last page of the CD booklet that accompanies the disc, there is a touching photograph from the 1950s, of baby Vince sitting in brother Bob's lap. Underneath it is the inscription "This album is dedicated to the memory of my brother, Bob. I hope I was half as good a little brother as he was a big brother."

Speaking about the evolution of his first Christmas album, Vince explained in March 1994 to readers of *Modern Screen's Country:* "I think it's a law that everyone has to do a Christmas album eventually. I enjoy Christmas records a lot, but I never really thought about doing one until I did a TV show called *Christmas in Washington* two years ago with Johnny Mathis, Anne Murray, and Anita Baker. . . . I thought, man, this is fun, something totally different than what I do all the time. So I wanted to show some reverence for where those tunes came from."

During that 1993 Christmas season, Vince began performing holiday songs on stage as well. Did any of them hit an emotional chord on stage? "The new song about my brother on the Christ-mas album hits home ['It Won't Be the Same This Year'] and the duet with my daughter ['Let There Be Peace on Earth']," he said to *Country Fever* in mid-1994. "Everything does for a different rea-son. 'When I Call Your Name' always will. I don't know that it's the greatest song I will ever record, but because of what it did for my career, that's always going to be my favorite song. . . . They're all part of the learning process. They're all part of the journey. It's the journey that's been more fun than becoming successful."

In addition to his Christmas album, Vince also released a Christmas music video entitled *Christmas with Vince Gill*, which was originally taped as a TNN cable TV special. He was joined by Chet Atkins, Amy Grant, Michael McDonald, the Tulsa Philhar-monic Orchestra, and the Oral Roberts University Chamber Singers. Highlights of the program included Amy Grant and Vince dueting on "Tennessee Christmas" and the entire cast performing "Rockin' Around the Christmas Tree."

Vince knew that he truly had a lot to be thankful for that holi-day season. He had watched his fan base grow and grow over the last year, and now his blossoming career continued to surprise him. With regard to his songwriting, and its evolution, Gill told *Country Fever* in 1994: "I'm not a real in-depth guy, writer wise. I like to write about what I'm feeling and try to make other people feel that too. I sat down with [Mary] Chapin [Carpenter] the other day. We talked about writing songs together, and she said, 'I don't understand how you can just make yourself do it in a couple-of-month period for a record.' I said, 'Let's just evaluate your lyrical content and mine.'. . . Mine is real simple but that's me; that's my personality. You see what you get. I'm easy going, and I sing to you how I feel. But that's why there are thirty-one flavors of ice cream."

At this point in his career, Vince's fame had definitely exceeded his expectations. Now that his concerts were more popular than ever, he had to manage his touring schedule carefully. In 1990 he performed 180 dates. In 1993 he did only 110 play dates. He had to admit that it was more exhausting now that he was a headliner and not an opening act. In addition, there were also photo shoots, press interviews, and television appearances to make. Nevertheless, year after year, he was managing to stay on top of it and have fun on stage at every show, and audiences responded to his infectious enthusiasm.

As 1993 ended, Vince Gill was sitting on top of the world. No longer did he have to push so hard with his career. The challenge now was to maintain his current level of success. "I have drive and ambition," he would explain to the *Los Angeles Times* in September 1994. "There are things that I'm intense about. I get on the guys [in my band] if they're not playing as good as they can and should. I want things to be the best. I'm a perfectionist. I want everyone else to be equally committed. I have a temper that shows up once in a while."

Having collected just about every music industry prize that was available to him, what was 1994 going to hold for him? More great music, more hits, more sold-out concerts, and more excitement. He was on a hot streak, and there were no signs of it ever cooling down.

EIGHT

WHEN LOVE FINDS YOU

For Vince Gill, 1994 was destined to be one full of awards and rewards. It was the year he made his movie debut, the year he stretched out stylistically into rhythm and blues and hardcore country, and the year he released one of the most successful albums of his career. It was also the year that he first collaborated on a CD with country singer Amy Grant.

On the record charts, Vince was continuing to pull hit singles off his 1992 *I Still Believe in You* album. In January 1994 his latest single, "Tryin' to Get Over You," entered the Top Forty, on its way to number one. That brought him a total of five number-one hits in less than two years.

Also in January of that year, at the American Music Awards, Vince took home the trophy for 1994 Country Single of the Year, for "Whenever You Come Around." Several weeks later, on March 1, 1994, at Radio City Music Hall where the Grammys were handed out, Vince, along with Asleep at the Wheel, and the other guest instrumentalists, were lauded with the award of the 1993 Best Country Instrumental Performance for "Red Wing" from the *Tribute to Bob Wills* album.

The Country Music Association continued their praises for his talent by giving Gill their accolades as their 1994 Male Vocalist of the Year, and honoring him and the other stars who contributed to *Common Thread: The Songs of the Eagles*, the winner of the 1994 Album of the Year. To top everything, they named Vince Gill the Entertainer of the Year. It didn't get much better than this!

Making jokes about the way Nashville gets all coifed and decked out for the Country Music Association Awards, Vince teased *TV Guide* in October 1994: "You get to see all of us dressed up, looking about as good as we ever will."

Speaking of his clean sweep of the awards in 1993, Gill claimed in the same publication, "I didn't mind it last year when I won all those awards. But it feels good just to get nominated. Simply going to the awards is nice. On top of that, I get the best parking spot, I get in for free, and I get to host. If I win anything, well 'yee-haw,' it's a bonus!"

Throughout 1994, Vince made several appearances on other talents' albums, including soundtracks, tribute albums, and guest-starring spots on the albums of friends. Two of these recordings, "Love Bug" and "A Farmer's Daughter," represent some of Vince's most old-school country songs to date.

"Love Bug" was recorded as part of George Jones's 1994 album, *The Bradley Barn Sessions* (MCA Records). Produced by Brian Ahern, the idea was to re-record several of the veteran star's biggest country hits as duets, or as group events. For instance, Trisha Yearwood was the guest on "Bartender's Blues," Alan Jackson sang "A Good Year for the Roses" with Jones, Keith Richards of the Rolling Stones played and sang on "Say It's Not You," and the trio of Emmylou Harris, Dolly Parton, and Trisha Yearwood joined George on "Where Grass Won't Grow." Vince Gill did a new duet rendition of Jones's 1965 Top Ten hit, "Love Bug." It is without a doubt the silliest, dumbest, and all-time corniest song that Gill has recorded to date.

On the other hand, "The Farmer's Daughter" from the Merle Haggard tribute album, *Mama's Hungry Eyes* (Arista Records,

1994), is, perhaps, the saddest, most maudlin, yet beautiful, straight country number Gill has ever recorded. Also on that disc is Brooks & Dunn providing the drinking song "Tonight the Bottle Let Me Down," Willie Nelson doing the sorrowful "Today I Started Loving Her Again," Pam Tillis watching "Silver Wings" pass, and Lorrie Morgan tackling the heartfelt "I Threw Away the Rose."

Vince's next foray in 1970s California rock came on the soundtrack from the rodeo film 8 *Seconds* (MCA Records, 1994). Originally the Phil Everly composition "When Will I Be Loved" was a Top Ten hit for the Everly Brothers, but it was in 1975 when Linda Ronstadt recorded it that she took it all the way to number one on the country chart, and number two on the pop chart. Vince's recording of "When Will I Be Loved" featured the harmony vocal of Karla Bonoffs, and it was produced by Andrew Gold and Kenny Edwards. (Gold, Edwards, and Bonoff were all veterans from the Linda Ronstadt camp. Kenny Edwards was part of Linda's first group, the Stone Poneys in the 1960s, and he and Andrew Gold both sang on Linda's recording of "When Will I Be Loved." Karla Bonoff was one of the prime supporting players on Ronstadt's 1976 album *Hasten Down the Wind,* as a background singer, the songwriter of "Lose Again," and the background singer/songwriter of "If He's Ever Near.")

In addition to being part of this album, Vince also appeared in the PG-13-rated feature, 8 *Seconds.* As the singer at the wedding reception, Gill literally has four seconds of screen time. This rodeo movie, starring Luke Perry and Stephen Baldwin, is an entertaining offering about champion bull riders. Portraying real life bull rider, the late Lane Frost, Perry brings the blood and guts and mud and sweat story dramatically and entertainingly to the screen. And, Vince looks great in this "don't-blink-or-you-will-miss-him" spot, where he is playing himself, essentially, with no lines, and only a brief establishment shot tuning his guitar.

Although the picture didn't become a hit, the critics seemed to like it. Bruce Williamson in *Playboy* magazine wrote, "Scores as a bull-busting Rocky!" And Bobbie Wugant at NBC-TV in Dallas called it "A crowd pleaser!"

Perhaps Gill's most exciting guest-starring appearance came on the 1994 album *Rhythm, Country and Blues* (MCA Records). A wonderful concept offering, it matched white country singers with black R&B stars to create a wonderful synthesis of both of their uniquely distinctive musical styles. The result proved to be a marvelously crafted project which yielded many excellent moments. Among the highlight duets on the album were Patti LaBelle and Travis Tritt singing "When Something Is Wrong with My Baby," Little Richard and Tanya Tucker pumping their limitless energy into "Something Else," the Pointer Sisters and Clint Black whipping their way through "Chain of Fools," Reba McEntire and Natalie Cole trying to out-croon each other on "Since I Fell for You," and Marty Stuart getting funky with the Staple Singers on "The Weight." Opening this brilliant concept disc is Gill and the exceptional Gladys Knight doing their version of the Ashford & Simpson-penned classic, "Ain't Nothing Like the Real Thing." (Originally, the song was a Top Ten smash at Motown Records for Marvin Gaye and Tammi Terrell in 1968.) This updating of the song is a smart matching of voices. Vince and Gladys are so good together on this cut that it wouldn't be out of the realm of possibility for the two of them to record a whole album of duets together.

On a sad note, this was to be the last album featuring veteran Conway Twitty. Twitty, who was one of Vince's favorite singing buddies, is heard here on a duet with Sam Moore of the legendary 1960s duo, Sam & Dave. Their version of "Rainy Night in Georgia" was one of several stand-out cuts on this release.

Gill's next career expansion came when he made his acting debut in the big-budgeted 1994 western spoof, *Maverick,* which starred Mel Gibson, Jodie Foster, and James Garner. In addition to the soundtrack album being a who's-who-of-Nashville event, several of the disc's contributors were given onscreen roles in the expensive movie as gamblers, rustlers, and thieves. Vince Gill was among them. He is seen wearing a stovepipe hat in one of the riverboat gambling scenes.

For the most part, the country star cameos are in the midst of the action, and, thus, have to be watched for carefully. In other words, a videotape player or a DVD player and a good "freeze frame" button are almost mandatory to find everybody. If you're quick, you can spot Hal Ketchum as a bank robber in the first part of the 129-minute, PG-rated movie. When the action shifts to the big riverboat gambling casino, Clint Black is front and center as a gambler who is caught cheating and is thrown overboard. There is a fast glimpse of Carlene Carter as a waitress with a tray of drinks. Right after James Garner drops his pistol on the floor, there is a brief closeup of Vince Gill, in his high-top hat and a scruffy beard, seen with his wife, Janis. Kathy Mattea and Waylon Jennings have a great little bit where they are trying to explain away the fact that they're carrying firearms. And, Gill's buddy, Patty Loveless, can be spotted when Jodie Foster folds her last losing hand at the gaming table. Vince's scene lasts mere seconds, but there he was—billed in the end credits and everything.

On the soundtrack album for the very popular *Maverick,* Vince is heard singing the Robbie Robertson composition, "Ophelia." Other 1990s Nashville stars who contributed to the disc included: Carlene Carter ("Something Already Gone"), Tracy

Lawrence ("Renegades, Rebels, and Rogues"), Clint Black ("A Good Run of Bad Luck"), Patty Loveless and Radney Foster ("The Rainbow Down the Road"), and Waylon Jennings ("You Don't Mess Around with Me"). The album finishes with an all-star rendition of "Amazing Grace." The Maverick Choir included Reba McEntire, Tammy Wynette, Amy Grant, Kathy Mattea, Restless Heart, Faith Hill, Billy Dean, Ricky Van Shelton, John Michael Montgomery, Eddie Rabbitt, and several more country stars.

—•—

It was in 1994 that thirty-six-year-old Vince and three-years-younger Amy Grant first collaborated in the recording studio. They had each contributed individual songs to the *Honeymoon in Vegas* soundtrack in 1992, but they had never recorded together. Amy had a huge following for her contemporary Christian recordings throughout the 1980s. With inspirational songs such as "Angels," "Raining on the Inside," and "Find a Way," she was virtually unknown to mainstream music fans, but she longed to break free of the constraints of that genre. She wanted to emulate the musical styles of several of her singing idols. According to Amy in the *Encyclopedia of Popular Music* (1989–98), "When I was in high school, I listened to Aretha Franklin and the Jackson Five. I remember discovering R&B music then and Joni Mitchell too."

Amy Grant had both the voice and the looks to appeal to a much wider audience, and in the early 1990s, at the age of thirty, she began forging ahead into the pop realm. Her first secular album, 1991's *Heart in Motion,* produced five chart hits, especially the number-one pop item "Baby Baby." *Heart in Motion* sold more than three million copies. Suddenly Grant's sights were set at bigger things than the tiny niche of contemporary Christian record buyers, and she never looked back. At the time, she was married to singer/songwriter Gary Chapman. The pair had met at a music industry party, after she had recorded his inspirational composition "My Father's Eyes."

Her follow-up album, *House of Love,* was scheduled for an August 1994 release date. According to Amy, it was her idea to request Gill to do the title cut duet with her. In *Billboard* magazine (July 30, 1994), Grant explained: "I asked Vince because he could hit the high notes." Reached for comment by the industry publication, Vince enthusiastically confirmed that he agreed to record the song with Amy, without even asking to hear it. "I just love Amy," he proclaimed.

Along with Melissa Etheridge and Don Henley of the Eagles, Vince was one of the stars on hand in 1994 to open the twenty-ninth Hard Rock Café, this one right in the middle of downtown Nashville. It is located down the street from the legendary Tootsie's Orchid Lounge, where Patsy Cline once had cocktails after appearances on the *Grand Ole Opry.* Now, like Vince Gill himself, downtown Nashville was truly a little bit of country and a little bit of rock 'n' roll.

In June 1994, Vince's new album, *When Love Finds You,* debuted, almost instantly selling millions of copies. It isn't surprising that this was to become his biggest-selling disc to date, because it finds Gill at the height of his game. He had found his voice vocally, and he had established a wonderful writing perspective which made his most insightful songs more touching than ever before. On this disc the slow songs are sadder and the faster songs more hook-laden.

On the leisurely side are songs such as the beautiful and heartfelt "Whenever You Come Around" and the sincere "When Love Finds You." On the doleful side of things nothing could be more melancholy than "Go Rest High on That Mountain," a song that can't be heard without giving you chills. And then, there are the up-tempo numbers such as "What the Cowgirls Do" and "You Better Think Twice," which are both memorable and exciting. Varied, and thoroughly pleasing throughout, this album showcases some of the best shadings of Vince's tenor voice and the most sensitive side of his songwriting. It is easy to appreciate why this is still the best-selling album of his career—to date.

On an intriguing note, this MCA album features one song that he wrote with Janis Gill, the first and only one found on any of his albums. The number is "Maybe Tonight," which concerns two friends contemplating an affair. Two songs earlier on the disc, he handles a song he wrote and sings with Amy Grant. It's interesting that this album should contain a song co-written with his wife, as well as one created with the woman Vince was later rumored to be linked with. Makes one wonder, doesn't it?

As to the guitar work on *When Love Finds You*, Vince observed in *Country Guitar* (Summer 1995) that it "surprised some people. I played it on a Les Paul [model guitar]—not your traditional country guitar. At the same time, when people come to see me live, they expect to hear the chicken pickin' stuff that I do. But then they walk away going, 'Well, he pulled out the Stratocaster and thought he was [Eric] Clapton.' But that's part of my thing. I really feel like I'm several different guitarists."

With regard to "You Better Think Twice," Vince revealed, in that same magazine interview, that his guitar inspiration on that cut came from Keith Richards of the Rolling Stones. "I basically used the tuning that Keith used on all those classic Stones songs such as 'Brown Sugar.' I removed the low E string and tuned the remaining strings to an open G chord, lowering the high E string down to D and the A string down to G." Choosing one of his most memorable highlights on this album, Vince claimed, "One of my favorites is 'Whenever You Come Around,' 'cause it's simple. It kind of mimics the melody of the tune, but the tone is really sweet. The older I get, the more I love how much 'less is more.' Sometimes the sweetest solos are not the most rippin' ones."

Probably the most talked about cut on *Where Love Finds You* was Gill's composition, "Go Rest High on That Mountain." It was dedicated to his late brother, Bob. The song idea was one he had had previously. In fact, Vince started writing the number when country singer Keith Whitley passed away in 1989. "I just kind of wrote the first verse right after Keith died, but it felt real awkward," Vince explained in *Country Music* for its March/April 1997 issue. "So I put it away and never touched it for four or five years. Then my older brother Bob passed away in 1993, and I knew I had to finish it. I felt then like I had a real valid reason for finishing the song."

On the subject of his late brother, Bob, Vince had told the *Star* tabloid in November 1993 of the song, "It's a way for me to write and grieve at the same time. Bob died of a heart attack. My mother found him in his house. I was sick for two weeks. I just shut down. . . . He had a pretty rough life. He had a car wreck when he was just about to graduate from college. He was going real fast and it was real bad. He was in a coma for three months not expected to live. . . . But he came out of it, probably not altogether like he'd been. . . . He'd forget to do things—like putting oil in his car. . . . So, he never really could find a great job. . . ."

In addition to the solid reputation he had on the charts in the mid-1990s for creating hits, Vince was also becoming quite an international sensation as well. For instance, when he was performing in Dublin, Ireland, the concertgoers suddenly began singing along as Gill did "I Still Believe in You." According to the star, he was amazed that a European audience would be so into his music that they knew the lyrics to all of his numbers and sang along. That was something he rarely witnessed with American audiences, so he was very pleasantly surprised.

On top of that, he was also getting another well-deserved reputation as a nice guy. According to his concert drummer Martin Pecker, speaking to the *Los Angeles Times* in the fall of 1994: "I'll tell you what kind of guy he is. I had rotator cuff surgery earlier this year, and he told me, 'Don't worry about it, take as long as you need, your job's here.' Anybody else in this business would have fired me. This is the best job there is. You know what our name for this tour is? It's the 'All Fun, No A**holes Tour.'"

Vince also reported that his wife, Janis, was spending more and more time at home and cutting back on her performances with Sweethearts of the Rodeo. "She likes it," Vince explained in *Country Fever* at the time. "It's not my decision. I've always told her, 'I married you and knew you were a guitar player and a singer. I didn't marry you to come and be my wife and all of a sudden not be a guitar player and a singer.' She could work as much as she wanted to. . . . I'm not a control freak. . . . She doesn't enjoy traveling as much as I do. I enjoy being on the bus and the camaraderie of those guys I travel with and playing and meeting people."

Explaining the dynamics of their marriage, Vince pointed out that when he first married Janis in 1980 and was a member of Pure Prairie League, he toured 245 dates a year. Throughout this period, their daughter, Jenny, witnessed a lot of coming and going with both her mom and dad. Show business was simply the Gills' business, and having either Vince or Janis missing from the family dinner table was nothing out of the ordinary for this household of three.

Discussing their marriage in a Fall 1994 special issue of *People* magazine entitled *People Country* in an article headlined "Vin (Not So) Ordinaire," Janis spoke about not being jealous of her husband traveling around the globe without her. Did she fear he was going to have an affair behind her back? According to her, "I have never worried about that. Ever. I have always trusted Vince. I know how tough it is. I know he's not out there partying. . . ." She also noted, "Wherever I go, all I get is, 'I'm so in love with your husband. You are sohhh lucky to be married to him. He is such a beautiful man.' What am I going to say? 'Shut up—I don't want you talking about my husband that way?' I just say, 'You're right. I am lucky.'"

In the same article, Vince strongly downplayed his so-called hunk image by stating, "I don't think my fan base looks at me as a heartthrob like some of these other guys."

He was also quick to point out that he and Janis were still as different as night and day: "Janis likes nice things—pretty things, furniture—more than I do," he revealed. "Nothing wrong with that. All I need when I'm home is a couch and a TV. I'd be fine living here on the golf course forever. But if she wants a mansion on the hill, I'll give her a mansion on the hill."

According to daughter Jenny, "He'll go down in the basement and blast his CDs."

Bewildered, family man Vince proclaimed, "I think I'm the only man in captivity whose daughter screams at him, 'Turn that thing down.'"

Often, when things become too frustrating, or, worse yet, too predictable, people reach out and rebel in different ways. This was also the year that Vince performed his most uncharacteristically rebellious act. Without notice, and just for a change of pace, he cut off all of his hair.

According to him, he sat down, put a towel around his shoulders, and grabbed a comb and a pair of hair clippers. While Janis looked on, he began giving himself his first home haircut. "It was pretty cool," he laughed about the experience in *New Country* magazine in 1996. "I did the sides first, then I cut a little higher and higher, and I said, 'You know, this isn't too bad!' because I still had all the hair on top. But when I took the strip down the middle, I sorta went, 'Oops!' It was pretty bizarre looking, but I was off [the road] and not really gonna do much, so it didn't seem like that big a deal." Vince had forgotten that he had an upcoming TV special to be taped at the Ryman Auditorium in Nashville a few weeks later, and here he was, suddenly bald. Reportedly, daughter Jenny let out a scream when she saw what her dad had done. And the folks at MCA Records nearly had a coronary attack.

"It was a major deal," Tony Brown proclaimed in the same magazine article. "In pop music, you can reinvent yourself several times and it always works. In country music, you can't do that, because it somehow seems to alienate people. So around the offices, everybody was treating it like somebody had died, like 'Have you seen Vince's hair? Man, he's bald-headed!'"

The funny thing was that when Tony finally saw the singer's new hairless hair style, he claims that he thought to himself, "He looks pretty damn cool! Everyone told me that I had to talk Vince into growing his hair back. So I told him, and I was laughing, 'Hey, Vince—everybody wants me to tell you to grow your hair back.'"

According to Brown, Gill said to him, "In that case, maybe I'll go back and cut it again."

According to his statements in *Country Music* magazine in the late winter of 1997: "It was pretty funny to see everybody flip out

Vince Gill has a reputation as the nicest guy in country music today. He is also known by his fans as one of the most talented musicians around. COURTESY OF GENE SHAW/STAR FILE

Left: Vince from his senior year at NW Classen High School in Oklahoma City. *Right*: Vince giving one of his earliest musical performances in a high-school program. COURTESY OF SETH POPPEL YEARBOOK ARCHIVES

Emmylou Harris and Vince Gill (*on left*), along with Ricky Skaggs (*right*), sing with country legend Bill Monroe (*center*), January 5, 1988. COURTESY OF ALAN L. MAYOR

Vince and his ex-wife, Janis, attending the 1995 Country Music Awards. She is one half of the country duo Sweethearts of the Rodeo. COURTESY OF ALAN L. MAYOR

Singing a duet with Patty Loveless at the Ryman Auditorium in Nashville. According to Vince, Patty is his all-time favorite singing partner. COURTESY OF SHEA SCULLIN

Dolly Parton and Vince Gill accepting their Country Music Association Award for the 1996 Vocal Event of the Year. COURTESY OF ALAN L. MAYOR

Left: Vince's duet with Gladys Knight, "Ain't Nothing Like the Real Thing," was one of the highlights of the album *Rhythm, Country and Blues.* COURTESY OF VINNIE ZUFFANTE/STAR FILE *Right:* If given the choice, Vince prefers a Hawaiian shirt to Western gear. COURTESY OF JOHN LEE/STAR FILE

Left: Steve Warner, Ricky Skaggs, and Vince Gill in the winner's circle at the Grammy Awards. COURTESY OF CHUCK PULIN/STAR FILE *Right:* Gill is part owner of a country theme restaurant in Los Angeles, along with Reba McEntire. COURTESY OF VINNIE ZUFFANTE/STAR FILE

Left: Vince picking up more awards from the Country Music Association, October 2, 1996. COURTESY OF SHEA SCULLIN *Right:* And the trophies just keep on coming—at the Country Music Association's 33rd annual awards. COURTESY OF SHEA SCULLIN

Vince Gill performing at a fund-raising event at Belmont University the day his guitar-playing hero, Bill Monroe, died. According to Vince, "I lost my mentor." As he struggled through tears, he sang his tribute song, "Go Rest High on That Mountain." COURTESY OF ALAN L. MAYOR

Left: Vince has more Grammy Awards than any other country artist in history. COURTESY OF VINNIE ZUFFANTE/STAR FILE *Right:* Vince's biggest passion—aside from music—is golf. COURTESY OF ALAN L. MAYOR

Vince at the Northern Telecom golf tournament in Tucson, Arizona. COURTESY OF MARK BEGO

Vince never intended to become a star vocalist. At the beginning of his career, it was his expressive guitar playing that ushered him into the world of country music. COURTESY OF ALAN L. MAYOR

the way they did. But it was also kind of sad, kind of sobering. It was like 'Doggone, I thought ya liked me for the way I sing, but I'm just a haircut to ya.' I remember I went out to the [Grand Ole] Opry to play a show, and [eighty-something veteran performer] Grandpa Jones hollered at me, 'Did'ja just git outta prison? Did'ja lose a bet!? . . .'

"There were actually several reasons I cut it. . . . I hate people to judge a book by its cover. I hate for people to be caught up in peer pressure, like they have to look a certain way. . . . I see these poor kids from Make-A-Wish [charity foundation] with cancer, and their hair's gone. . . . Well, I just wanted to be able to say to them, 'Hey, I'm pretty popular, and my hair's gone!'

"I also wanted to show my kid, she's fourteen years old and goin' through the peer pressure thing. . . . This was kind of a way to teach her that just because somebody tells you that you might ought try something [such as drinking, smoking, and so on] doesn't mean you should."

According to Vince, it was a bit of a relief to spend months at a time never worrying about what his hair looked like or having to deal with it. He also joked that the new style saved him money on shampoo. Actually, people were so shocked over his new bald look that it enabled him to pretend that he wasn't really Vince Gill. "The funny thing was, I was just goofin' off," he said in *New Country* magazine in 1996. "We have cars come by the house a lot, taking pictures, and if I'm around I'll go out and wave, whatever. So I walked out to the driveway one day, the neighbors across the street were signaling, 'Get back in! Get back in!'. . . that there was somebody out there, you know? So, just for fun, I started going [in a hillbilly accent] 'Git outta hyar! He didn't leeuv heer no mawr! We bawt his howse!' I was definitely just spoofin' these people, and then I hear this woman scream, 'We always heard you were so nice!' and they drove off."

In 1994, Vince Gill was among the first inductees into the newly founded Oklahoma Country-Western Hall of Fame. Also on the list were Bob Wills and Bob Wood. (Wood is a record store owner in Oklahoma City who is something of a local legend.) The Oklahoma Country-Western Hall of Fame and Museum plays host to thousands of visitors yearly. Located in the community of Del City, southeast of downtown Oklahoma City, it has a display of Vince Gill memorabilia, as well as salutes to Reba McEntire and Garth Brooks.

Now that the money was rolling in from Vince's hit recordings, he began to diversify his investments. With that in mind, in August 1994, the doors opened on the Country Star Restaurant in Los Angeles amid the Universal Studios City Walk. Vince, along with Reba McEntire, Wynonna Judd, and TNN's *Crook & Chase* talk-show hosts Lorraine Crook and Charlie Chase, became the owners of this newly constructed theme restaurant. Because Universal City is a huge shopping and entertainment area—Hollywood style—the Country Star Restaurant is oversized too. With 14,000 square feet of floor area, visitors enter the restaurant through a large forty-two-foot-tall lighted jukebox.

Along the lines of the Hard Rock Café, the Motown Café, and Planet Hollywood, the Country Star Restaurant is stocked with country memorabilia from its celebrity owners, including one of Wynonna's prize Harley Davidson motorcycles. The cuisine served there is country style with a West Coast twist. The barbecued ribs are excellent, as are the specialties on the menu including coconut fried chicken, Texas onion pie, and, of course, the fried catfish. Not only was he "cookin'" on the music charts, but Vince was also serving up his share of country cooking as well. Among the stars who came out to sample the restaurant's fare at its gala opening were actor Gary Busey, rock legend Little Richard, country queen Loretta Lynn, and comedian Sinbad.

As 1994 came to a close, alongside other major chart-toppers such as George Strait, Reba McEntire, Wynonna Judd, Garth Brooks, and Alan Jackson, Vince Gill was now one of the undisputed superheroes of 1990s country music. Unfortunately, even superheroes sometimes falter. At least Vince's didn't share the same fate as several legendary heroes of ancient history—such as Samson. When Delilah cut off Samson's hair, he found that he had lost all of his strength. In Vince Gill's case, when he sheered off all his own hair, his superhero singing talents were all safely intact, as he prepared to make 1995 one of his best years yet on the country music sales charts

NINE

HIGH LONESOME SOUND

The year 1995 began much like the previous two, with Vince Gill winning the music industry's top trophies, one after another. For the string of hit recordings he was producing, each award was a well-deserved one. On March 1, 1995, at the Shrine Auditorium in Los Angeles, Vince found himself competing in the category of Best Country Vocal Performance, Male, for a Grammy Award. His 1994 song "When Love Finds You" was competing against "Thinkin' Problem" by David Ball, "Your Love Amazes Me" by John Berry, "I Swear" by John Michael Montgomery, and "Pocket of a Clown" by Dwight Yoakam. Vince won his sixth Grammy that night. It was beginning to become an annual habit with him.

When the BMI Songwriter's Awards were handed out that same year, Gill was named their Songwriter of the Year. At the Nashville Music Awards, Gill was heralded as their Male Vocalist of the Year, and they gave their Song of the Year trophy to "Go Rest High on That Mountain." To top it all off, the Country Music Association bestowed their prestigious Male Vocalist of the Year prize on Vince as well.

As the year progressed, Gill continued to pull one hit single after another from his *When Love Finds You* album. In February

1995, "Which Bridge to Cross (Which Bridge to Burn)" entered the Top Forty, on its way to number four on Billboard's music industry charts. In May, "You Better Think Twice" entered the Top Forty, ultimately peaking at number two.

Meanwhile, Dolly Parton was working in the recording studio with producer Steve Buckingham, who had previously produced all of the Sweethearts of the Rodeo albums while they were at Columbia Records. When Dolly signed a recording contract with Columbia in the late 1980s, part of their agreement was that she would alternate albums: one country, one pop, one country, one pop, and so forth. *Something Special,* which was released in 1995, was marketed in both directions, although the overall sound was pop/adult contemporary. It became a Top Ten disc on the Country Albums chart, and peaked at number fifty-four on the 200 Albums chart. On the *Something Special* disc, she positioned herself as more of a torch and contemporary singer than as a country performer. She is heard on several touching ballads, including "Crippled Bird" and the poignant "Change." She also chose to re-record two of her most famous signature songs: "I Will Always Love You" and "Jolene." All of the songs on the album were written by Dolly herself.

Dolly had just made a fortune in 1992 when Whitney Houston recorded Parton's composition "I Will Always Love You," included it in the box-office megahit film *The Bodyguard,* and turned her rendition of the number into one of the biggest hits of the decade.

Dolly herself had gotten a lot of mileage in the past out of "I Will Always Love You." She originally recorded it in 1974 and turned it into a number-one hit on the country charts. Then, when she starred in the 1982 film *Best Little Whorehouse in Texas,* she insisted on including the song in the movie, and again she turned it into a number-one hit. Finally, when Whitney Houston turned it into a new massive success, which sat at number one for fourteen weeks and sold more than four million copies, it became one of the most successful songs in the history of recorded music. Not one to let a good thing die, Parton decided to re-record the song for her forthcoming *Something Special* album.

Because Dolly had already recorded the song twice as a solo performance, she felt she had to put a fresh twist on the offering. The new turn she gave it was to have Vince Gill record it with her as a duet.

According to a 1997 book entitled *Three Chords and the Truth* by Laurence Leamer, this caused a very big problem between MCA Records and Columbia Records.

"Would you come and sing with me on 'I Will Always Love You' for my new album?" Dolly said to Vince when she personally telephoned him. Gill agreed, and MCA had no problem with it, so long as it was just an album cut and not a single. At the time MCA was still pulling singles off his *When Love Finds You* album, and they were getting ready to release "Go Rest High on That Mountain" as a single.

Dolly telephoned Vince again, thanked him for doing the song, and suggested that the recording would make a wonderful single.

Gill assured her that he was behind her, whatever she wanted to do with the recording. When the album was released, country radio stations across the country began playing "I Will Always Love You." Simultaneously, MCA had just released Vince's "Go Rest High on That Mountain," and they were busy promoting it. Legally speaking, MCA could have demanded that "I Will Always Love You" be withdrawn as a single, but Vince interceded and asked his label to just let the singles fall where they might. In that way, both songs ended up becoming hits.

At the time, Dolly did all she could to promote the album. She announced in a *Country Weekly* cover story (August 29, 1995): "One of the things that made this album really special is I did 'I

Will Always Love You' as a duet for the first time with none other than Vince Gill. . . . He did such a beautiful job and I was so honored that he even wanted to sing it," she modestly said. It was also the big buildup to her January 1996 fiftieth birthday, so she was determined to turn the song into a hit.

The final outcome found "I Will Always Love You" peaking on *Billboard* magazine's Hot Country Singles and Tracks at number fifteen and "Go Rest High on That Mountain" topping at number fourteen. Music industry followers noted that "Go Rest High on That Mountain" had a built-in problem. It seemed that country radio stations were hesitant to play a song about death, no matter how masterful or touching it was. They certainly had a point. It's not the kind of number you necessarily want to hear again and again on your car radio. It isn't exactly a "feel good" song.

Despite "Go Rest High on That Mountain" being very low-key and somber, there was a music video produced of the song. It featured Vince on an empty stage in a theater singing the lead part, and then joined by his harmony singing buddies, Patty Loveless and Ricky Skaggs. On a projection screen behind them, beautiful photography of cloudy skies and majestic mountain tops were projected. It emerged a very tasteful and visually exciting video, even if the subject matter is one of stark mortality.

With regard to "Go Rest High on That Mountain," Vince found that it had a profound effect on many people. It became known as such a touching and sentimental song of loss that the title has even been engraved on cemetery stones, as a final tribute.

The spring of 1995 was when the tragic bombing of a federal office building in downtown Oklahoma City occurred. Vince was especially upset and frightened by this appalling crime, because his mother, Jerene, worked in Oklahoma City very near the devastated site. When he heard the horrific news of the tragedy, he immediately tried to reach his mother to find out if she was safe.

According to him in *Star* (May 16, 1995): "My mom worked a couple of blocks away, and I couldn't find anybody because all the phone lines were dead. I called Larry Fitzgerald, who's my manager, and he had spoken to my mother shortly after it happened. She was at home, and everything was OK." Relieved to learn that news, Vince donated the proceeds from several of his upcoming concerts toward the relief fund for the families of the victims.

In 1995, Vince Gill had three separate new "greatest hits" albums in the stores. RCA Records released a beautifully packaged twenty-cut retrospective of his recordings called *The Essential Vince Gill*. Several of the tracks on the album are songs that had not appeared on his original three RCA albums. In addition to this, Polygram produced *The Best of Pure Prairie League*, featuring nine cuts with Vince Gill as the lead singer and contributing band member. The really big news, however, was his MCA hits package, *Souvenirs*, which hit number three on the Country Albums chart and number eleven on the 200 Albums chart. Ultimately, it sold more than two million copies and is a brilliant retrospective of his first five years of hits at MCA Records. It contained his five number-one hits and a nice variety of cuts from albums other than his own. *Souvenirs* included the important songs, "The Heart Won't Lie" with Reba McEntire, "I Will Always Love You" with Dolly Parton, and "I Can't Tell You Why" from *Common Ground: The Songs of the Eagles*.

Also in 1995, Vince was one of the guest performers who contributed his time in the studio to a strangely eclectic album called *One Voice*, which was released the following year by MCA Records, in time for the 1996 Olympics to be held in Atlanta, Georgia. Although country-oriented in sound, it was stylistically all over the map. On the disc Vince is heard instrumentally on the first track of the album, entitled "Atlanta Reel '96." Clearly an homage to the classic Virginia Reels of the 1800s, "Atlanta Reel

'96" was written by producer Michael Omartian, whom Gill had worked with on the song "Ophelia" from the film *Maverick.*

On the *One Voice* album, the song "Atlanta Reel '96" is performed by Michael Omartian (piano), and features Vince Gill (electric guitar), Chet Atkins (electric guitar), Alison Krauss (fiddle), Bela Fleck (banjo), and Paul Franklin (pedal steel guitar).

With regard to "Atlanta Reel '96," in 1995 Vince reported to *Country Guitar* magazine: "I feel that I get to showcase my playing on my records to a certain extent. At the same time, I'm smart enough to know that the majority of the people don't want to hear guitar soloing. . . . I just worked on an instrumental piece with Michael Omartian that's hopefully going to be the theme for the '96 Olympics. . . . Chet Atkins, Alison Krauss, and Paul Franklin [pedal steel guitar] were also on it."

Also starring on the *One Voice* album are a squad of Vince Gill's buddies and singing partners. Amy Grant and Patty Loveless offer a duet version of the song "Every Kinda People," which is pure contemporary pop/jazz. Trisha Yearwood goes for high drama on "The Flame." Karla Bonoff, who sang with Vince on "When Will I Be Loved" from 8 *Seconds,* duets with the Nitty Gritty Dirt Band on the ballad "You Believed in Me." Mark O'Connor provides a classical fiddle concerto with the Concordia Orchestra on his self-composed "The Fiddle Concerto." By far, the most curious and incomparably impressive song on the album is the trio of Nanci Griffith, Donna Summer, and Raul Malo (of the Mavericks), singing a multilingual version of Julie Gold's "From a Distance," which, earlier, Bette Midler had turned into a hit. Not only is it fun to hear Raul's Spanish and Donna Summer's German, but you can't believe how wonderfully these three voices blend together.

On October 16, 1995, Vince was one of the stars to tee off for VH1 cable TV's Second Annual Fairway to Heaven golf tournament.

The event, which was held at Tournament Players Club at Sumerlin in Las Vegas, also featured such all-star golfers as Bruce Hornsby, Graham Nash, Smokey Robinson, and Stephen Stills. They were also joined on the links with such PGA pro golfers as Helen Alfredsson, John Daly, Roger Maltbie, Steve Pate, Larry Rinker, and Ted Tryba.

As 1996 began, it was time for Vince to rack up another batch of industry awards. On February 28, when the Grammy Awards were presented at the Shrine Auditorium in Los Angeles, Vince was nominated in the category of 1995 Best Country Song (Songwriter's Award) for "Go Rest High on That Mountain." Also in that category were "Any Man of Mine" (Robert John "Mutt" Lange and Shania Twain songwriters, Shania Twain artist), "Gone Country" (Bob Dill songwriter, Alan Jackson artist), "I Can Love You Like That" (Maribeth Derby, Steve Diamond, Jennifer Kimball songwriters, John Michael Montgomery artist), and "You Don't Even Know Who I Am" (Gretchen Peters songwriter, Patty Loveless artist).

In the category of 1995 Best Country Vocal Performance, Male, Vince was again tapped for "Go Rest High on That Mountain." His competition included "Standing on the Edge of Goodbye" by John Berry, "Gone Country" by Alan Jackson, "I Can Love You Like That" by John Michael Montgomery, and "A Thousand Miles from Nowhere" by Dwight Yoakam. That evening, Gill took both of those prestigious awards, giving him Grammys number seven and eight for his growing collection.

When the TNN/*Music City News* Awards were given out in 1996, "Go Rest High on That Mountain" won an award as Best Vocal Collaboration as recorded by Vince, with harmony vocals by Patty Loveless and Ricky Skaggs. At the BMI Songwriter's Awards, they saluted Vince for 1996's Most Performed Songs: "Which Bridge to Cross (Which Bridge to Burn)" and "You Better Think Twice." In addition, BMI presented Vince with their 1996 Humanitarian Award for his charity work.

Saluting Gill for his accomplishments the previous year, the Nashville Music Awards declared him the 1995 Male Vocalist of the Year, and they named "Go Rest High on That Mountain" the 1995 Song of the Year. When the Country Music Association Awards were handed out later in 1996, they chose "Go Rest High on That Mountain" the Song of the Year. Even more exciting was the fact that they selected "I Will Always Love You" by Dolly and Vince as the 1996 Vocal Event of the Year.

Gill continued to glean a reputation in and around Nashville as the nicest guy in town. For example, in 1996 when Patty Loveless's guitar player took a weekend off when his wife had a baby, Patty was left in a lurch. No problem. Vince simply volunteered to fill in on guitar at her concert. As he explained later, it was sheer pleasure to spend time with his buddy Patty Loveless, and he had fun being on stage without having to entertain the crowd by talking and making jokes in between performing.

On September 11, 1996, Vince was one of the country stars on hand to pay his respect to bluegrass music pioneer, Bill Monroe, age eighty-four, who had passed away two days previously. At the event a crowd of several of Bill's superstar friends and admirers gathered at the Ryman Auditorium in Nashville to pay tribute to him and his lengthy, memorable life in song. Emmylou Harris performed "Wayfaring Stranger," Connie Smith sang "How Great Thou Art," Ricky Skaggs interpreted Monroe's "Rawhide," and Vince Gill offered his fitting "Go Rest High on That Mountain."

During 1996, RCA Records released a ten-song album of Vince Gill material entitled *Vince Gill: Super Hits*. It contained several of his early successes: "Everybody's Sweetheart," "Cinderella," and

"The Radio." The real news, however, was the debut of the previously unreleased song "Savannah (Don't You Ever Think of Me)" and the CD debut of "Baby It's Tough." "Baby It's Tough" has a great all-male chorus, which is meant to replicate the work that the Jordanaires did with Elvis Presley. It is a long-forgotten, fun track.

In addition to all of the awards that the multitalented Mr. Gill was collecting, the really big happening was the most stylistically creative album of his recording career: the New Orleans Cajun-flavored *High Lonesome Sound*. Ultimately selling a million copies, and making it to number three on the Country Album chart in *Billboard,* this album represents Vince's reaching out into exciting new directions, and many of his biggest fans claim that it is by far the best album of his career to date.

According to Steve Morse of the *Boston Globe*: "Gill widened his repertory on the new disc, *High Lonesome Sound*. He demonstrates what many fans have known for a long time, namely that Gill is a well-rounded musician who respects country's roots, but also isn't afraid to rock out."

Explaining the evolution of the album in *New Country* magazine in 1996, Vince pondered first about inspiration: "I'd gone to the well plenty," he says, "not that it's a bad well at all. . . . I felt like my records were getting a little similar. And I'm musical enough to want to do some different things, but not in such a drastic way that I turn my back on everything I've accomplished—that's not the exercise."

When it had come time to select material to include on *High Lonesome Sound,* Vince pondered in that same article: "Well, let's see what you can come up with—kinda reinvent yourself. And if I got criticized in my work, it was always like, 'Well, your live show is pretty exciting, but that doesn't come across on record.' But I'm not out to prove to the world that I'm a great guitar player, and I'm not out to prove that on this new record either. You know, it's hard to strike a balance between pleasing myself a little but not going too far."

Comparing the earlier *When Love Finds You* to *High Lonesome Sound,* Gill said to *Country Weekly* magazine (August 18, 1998): "The last record, I would say, had something to do with it. I'm real proud of the last record. I made that record like I wanted to make it and it did quite well and had hits and won Grammys and all the things that are great, you know, but I didn't feel the enthusiasm."

According to Vince in the *San Diego Union Tribune* in 1996: "I tried to make this a more musically satisfying album. I know there's stuff on there that's not unlike the stuff I've done before, so I'm not worried about not getting on the radio. I just did some things on the record that I don't intend to get on the radio. I don't have a desire to have a hit record with a song that's real weird. It's just me having some fun. It's nothing earth-shattering, I assure you. It's just different—for me. And I don't have to do a whole album of it to be content."

What was it that made the highly successful artist go in the direction of experimentation? Interestingly enough, it was singer Amy Grant who gave him the most encouragement, in a roundabout way. In that same interview Vince said, "The honest answer is that I've become really good buddies with Amy Grant. She's getting ready to make a new record, and she said: 'I'm making a new LP and feel like doing something different.' And I said, 'Hey, is your farm paid for?' And she said: 'Yes.' So, I said: 'Then do it!' So, I kind of took my own advice, which is really scary. Never take my advice! Never!" he laughed.

The album *High Lonesome Sound* kicks into full gear with its very first cut. Sounding more Doobie Brothers than Gill-meister, Vince rocks out on his composition "One Dance with You." A peppy rocking dance number, "One Dance with You" gets the party going, already unlike any ballad-dominated Vince album before. Next up is the first version of his composition "High Lonesome Sound," set to a pop/bluegrass/folk/rock arrangement, with Alison

Krauss delivering vocal accompaniment. Of this version, Vince claimed in *Country Weekly* (March 3, 1998): "It's like a cross between Bill Monroe and Stevie Wonder. It got really good, funky and bluesy real quick in a real neat way."

The next cut on *High Lonesome Sound* is the emotional ballad "Pretty Little Adriana," which is one of Vince's finest writing moments to date. Although it can be interpreted as a song about a pining lover, it in fact is about the death of a little girl named Adriana. According to Vince in *Country Music* (March/April 1997): "There was a little girl named Adriana Dickerson about twelve years old who was killed in Nashville in a drive-by shooting. I don't think they ever really found out how or why. She was just the prettiest little girl, and it really shook up the whole city in a big way. I kind of wrote the song from her parents' point of view. If you listen to the song from that perspective, all of a sudden it's very different from what you first perceived it to be. . . . I'm not trying to explain everything so everybody does get it. I love for people to listen to music and find their own meanings."

Just to lighten things up a bit, in the fourth cut ("A Little More Love") Vince sings about keeping a love affair alive to a rocking beat. But, on the next selection, he moves the proceedings to Bourbon Street for the Mardi Gras–flavored "Down to New Orleans." The background vocals on this scorcher of a Southern rocker are provided by the very torchy Bekka Bramlett. The effect is excitingly explosive. This song is a whole new Vince Gill high point. He has sung of "Savannah" in the past, and he romanticized "Oh Carolina," but, this third salute to a Southern city is by far the finest.

Having Bekka Bramlett on "Down to New Orleans," and the following cut, "Tell Me Lover," was just the inspired move Gill needed. She brought a special, smoldering excitement to "Down to New Orleans." Speaking of Bekka, Vince would say in *Country Music* in the winter issue of 1998: "That's as inspirational as anything I've done in my life—hearing Bekka's voice over the microphone and on the record. This is the honest-to-God truth—there wasn't a practice run. The first time she opened her mouth, it just totally blew me away. It was the most impressive studio performance I've ever heard. I picked up my chair, threw it out [of] the studio, jumped up and down, and started dancing."

Although she hasn't had a lot of solo success at this point, Bekka Bramlett is a second generation rocker. She is the daughter of Delaney Bramlett and Bonnie Bramlett Sheridan, better known as the 1960s duo and band: Delaney and Bonnie & Friends. They scored several big hits including "Never Ending Song of Love," "Free the People," and "Only You Know and I Know." With a revolving cast of characters, the "& Friends" included from time to time: Eric Clapton, Leon Russell, Rita Coolidge, Duane Allman, and Dave Mason. TV viewers will recognize Bekka's mom as Bonnie Sheridan, who played a waitress on TV's *Roseanne* for several seasons in the 1990s.

Bekka took over Stevie Nicks's place in Fleetwood Mac in the 1990s, for the album *Time* (Warner Bros. Records, 1995), which also included Dave Mason. After the original configuration of Fleetwood Mac got back together in 1997, Bekka joined with another Fleetwood alumnus, Billy Burnette, and recorded a Nashville album under the name of Bekka & Billy.

"Tell Me Lover," from the *High Lonesome Sound* album, which features Bekka in the background, is a scorcher too. Considering that it has to be the first country song to ask the urban tinged musical question, "Waz up with you?" clearly Vince was moving into new territory.

The next entry, "Given More Time," written with Don Schlitz, was another stylistic change for Vince in which he experimented with rhythm, breaking away from his established mode. It is helped by the use of an accordion and fiddle. The effect is great, and the song is the perfect ode to Gill's days as a California rocker in the 1970s, when groups such as Little Feat and Steely Dan ruled the rock world. For harmony vocals on that particular cut, Vince chose Patty Loveless. As usual, their voices blended as well on California rock 'n' roll, as they do on country.

One of the album's most beautiful items is "You and You Alone," which Vince sings with Shelby Lynne. It is a very strong love song with a neat opening musical signature.

Next to "Pretty Little Adriana," the album's most downbeat song is the ballad "World's Apart," which Vince co-authored with Bob DiPietro, who is Pam Tillis's husband. The line in this song about there being nothing sadder than when children leave home, and the memory is of yesterday, makes this entry truly heart melting. Again, Vince proves the master of sad ballads.

A more upbeat sentimental favorite is Gill's version of his railroad composition, "Jenny Dreamed of Trains," written nearly a decade earlier with Guy Clark. Naturally, it is the telling of a real-life narrative about his daughter. It was recorded in the past by Sweethearts of the Rodeo, and by Mary Chapin Carpenter. Vince's rendition is especially touching.

The last cut on the album was the totally countrified version of the title cut, featuring the bluegrass band Union Station, with Alison Krauss. Vince said in *Country Weekly* magazine: "Bill originated the phrase 'High Lonesome Sound' and I love it. This is a real tribute to him. He's one of the strongest men that's ever been. But he's getting on up there in age, and, unfortunately, that's what's waiting for all of us."

The title cut, "High Lonesome Sound," ended up with two completely different versions on the LP. The initial one, with bluegrass diva Alison Krauss and her band, Union Station, is a straight-out tribute to the classic country sound of Bill Monroe. The second version of the song sounds more like Stevie-Wonder-goes-Nashville.

Describing how the song "High Lonesome Sound" appeared on the album twice, Vince explained in *New Country* in 1996: "The thing was, we were gonna do that cut just bluegrass, with Alison [Krauss] and her band [Union Station]. We hadn't even planned on cutting that song with my band. Then we wound up with a few extra hours one day, and I said, 'Hey, just for grins, let's track it and see what happens!'" Vince put the band version on the album—with Alison singing harmony vocal—as the second cut, and then used the Alison Krauss & Union Station version to close the disc.

Of all of the singers with whom Vince has sung over the years, he feels that Alison Krauss has one of the most distinctive sounds in the business. "I remember the first time I heard Alison sing, and thinking, 'Boy, that's about as pure as a voice can get!' Alison's a lot like me—she's about bein' in a band, and I respect her for sticking to her guns. That's why I had her whole band and not just her play on the song," he said in *Country Music* magazine in early 1997.

With such a wealth of background and harmony singers available to him, how does he make his selections when it is time to go into the recording studio? As he told *Country Weekly* in 1998: "I hear a song and I hear Shelby Lynne singing—or Alison, who has the purest voice. I try to line up what I hear in my head. I feel like it's my time to pretend I'm like a casting director in a movie."

How did Vince's guitar playing differ on "High Lonesome Sound"? According to him, "I turned my guitar up louder. I wanted to be more adventuresome in the grooves and feel of these songs. They're all different from anything I've ever done—and with them feeling as different as they do, it makes my guitar-playing different than it has been."

One of the big differences between *High Lonesome Sound* and all of Vince's previous albums is the fact that, for the first time, he wrote every single song on this album—either alone, or with collaborators. In this way, this album is much more of a personal project for him.

Most interesting to note is the fact that Janis Gill was nowhere to be found on the *High Lonesome Sound* album, neither in background vocal, nor mention in the liner notes. Also, it was significant that, when Sweethearts of the Rodeo made a new album that year, entitled *Beautiful Lies* and released by the independent Sugarhill Records label, it was the first offering by that group not to have Vince appear on it in some capacity.

Pairing these events with a careful examination of the lyrics to Gill's song "World's Apart," it wouldn't take a genius to figure out that he was obviously singing this song of isolation about his marriage to Janis, which was just about to hit the domestic rocks.

During this threshold year Janis and her sister Kristine started their own dress shop in Nashville called the Gill & Arnold Boutique, located at 334 Main Street in Franklin, Tennessee. Reportedly, Janis bankrolled the store with $700,000 from the Gills' savings. For a long time, Janis longed to design her own Sweethearts of the Rodeo fashions, and with the opening of the shop she seized the chance.

While Janis was keeping herself busy in Nashville, Vince was increasingly out on the road. There were some who said that this was the factor that put the most strain on their marriage. When Bob Allen of *Country Music* (March/April 1997) asked him if he missed being at home with Janis and Jenny, Gill replied, "Oh, yeah, sure. You know that Alabama song, 'In Pictures'? I well up every time I hear that. I do get to spend a great amount of time at home with my kid, but I wanta be there every second. I don't wanta miss a thing. . . . On the other hand, a lot of the folks who do get to go home every night would sit here and say, 'Man, I wish I could do what you do: cruise around on that bus and watch movies and drink beers after the show and hang out and have fun and travel and play golf every day. And, I do have a great life. I don't think there's a living soul out there I'd trade places with."

———

Vince also released his third video compilation in 1996. Entitled *Souvenirs—Live at the Ryman,* it is essentially him performing fifteen of his biggest 1990s hits live in concert. His performance was taped in Nashville at the historic Ryman Auditorium, famous as the original site of the radio edition of the Grand Ole Opry. In addition to his greatest 1990s hits, Gill also does "Buck's Run" and "Jenny Dreamed of Trains" in this entertaining two-hour presentation. This video program was also aired on TNN cable as a television special.

In December 1996 Vince embarked on his first-ever Christmas tour, working with a full orchestra. His guest conductor for this trek was his producer friend Michael Omartian, who not only worked with Vince and with Amy Grant, but had also produced music for Cher, Donna Summer, Rod Stewart, Michael Bolton, and Whitney Houston. Said Omartian at the time on the music news Web site, *Internet News Service:* "I consider it an honor to be part of this concert series." According to Vince on the same site: "There is nothing more beautiful than being lucky enough to stand and sing in front of an orchestra. And the possibility of seeing my band in tuxedos is beyond words!"

In 1996 and 1997, Vince scored one Top Ten hit after another with singles from the *High Lonesome Sound* album. They included "Pretty Little Adriana," "World's Apart," "A Little More Love," and "You and You Alone."

Although Gill's career was going strong, speculation about a strain in his marriage was running rampant in Nashville. It seemed like he and Janis were pretty much living separate lives at this point in time. Part of the obvious stress was evident in Vince's weight. He had gained several pounds and was looking much heavier than he had only five years before. He was beginning to appear more "good ole boy" chunky around the middle, than the GQ-toned hunk depicted on his *I Still Believe in You* (1992) album. Packing on the extra weight was a sure signal to many that something was wrong in the Gill household.

The February 1997 Grammy Awards were held in a different venue than usual. Not only was the ceremony staged in New York City, but for the first time in its history, it was broadcast live from Madison Square Garden. When the trophies were handed out, Vince won two prizes: the Best Country Vocal Performance, Male, for the song "Worlds Apart," and the Best Country Collaboration with Vocals for the song "High Lonesome Sound" with Alison Krauss & Union Station. Gill attended the awards with his wife, Janis. This was to be one of their last public appearances together.

For this award spectacular, the Gills were in Madison Square Garden—famed for boxing matches. And it was reportedly the site of one of their final marital battles. Although Vince was again in the winner's circle on stage, Janis apparently took offense at something. According to *Star* newspaper, Janis left her husband's side midway through the proceeding. The *Star* (May 6, 1997) later reported that a guest ran into Janis—who was on her way out of the auditorium. "Aren't you going to stay and celebrate with Vince?" the individual asked Janis. A curt Mrs. Gill apparently snapped back, "No. I've already seen enough."

The same tabloid article quoted Janis Gill as having said in February 1997: "I just miss Vince so much and I would really like to spend more time with him. I've had some very difficult times in my marriage, like anybody else."

After months of speculation, on April 17, 1997, Vince released an official statement on his divorce, later published in *People* magazine (May 5, 1997), proclaiming that it was "a private and personal matter. And, and with all due respect, I would like to keep it that way."

Throughout the spring of 1997, the marital status of Vince and Janis Gill was big news in the tabloids. On tour with Bekka Bramlett in his band, she (age twenty-nine) and Vince (age forty) were romantically linked—at least speculatively. In *Star* (May 6, 1997) "a source" was credited with saying: "Bekka was Vince's release valve while his home life has been going up in smoke. She's a great girl and she's not a home-wrecker—she never even hooked up with Vince until his marriage got into serious trouble. But now she's the apple of his eye."

Interestingly enough, the only major recording on which Vince appeared, at the time, was as a guitar player on Bekka's debut album as a duet with Billy Burnette. The honky-tonk sound of the *Bekka & Billy* album (Uni Records, 1997) also featured Bekka's dad, Delaney Bramlett, and garnered good reviews. More press was generated by Bekka's relationship with Vince, however, than by her album.

The *National Enquirer* (May 6, 1997) quickly jumped into the act, claiming that Vince confided in a friend, "I didn't want it to end, but with all the fighting over the years, I guess it was meant to be. I've given it my all—there's just nothing more I can do." The article, which was entitled, "Wife's Nasty Anniversary Gift to Vince Gill: a Divorce!" quoted another "insider" as saying, "Vince is brokenhearted. He's tried everything to hold his marriage together, even seeing marriage counselors over the years. But, nothing worked."

People magazine dispatched a reporter to Canada to catch Vince in concert in Ottawa. The journalist noted that the April 19,

1997, concert contained an especially poignant version of the song "I Still Believe in You," which was filled with irony. The number had originally been written by Gill about spatting and then making up with Janis. A reconciliation was impossible now. The same article of May 5, 1997, reported that one concertgoer was overheard when the show was over, saying: "Wasn't that the saddest show you ever saw?"

That spring, *New Country* magazine harped on the country star about the divorce, asking if it put a dent in his previously perfect "nice guy" armor? "I guess, but at the same time it's kind of ironic, because I'm not the one standing here blowing my own horn. . . . I've got just as many flaws as anybody else. You can read what you want about people, but these are my shoes, and I walk in 'em. . . . No, my life's not perfect, and it has elements that I struggle with. But whatever happens to me, I screw up or do this or do that, I have to close my eyes and sleep at night and live with myself, and that's always gonna be the bottom line for me."

While all of the divorce talk was being bantered around at the newsstands and on the air, Vince had marked his fortieth birthday on April 12, 1997. With regard to this milestone birthday, Vince calmly said in *Country Weekly* magazine: "I didn't look at it as achieving a goal. I just enjoy playing and singing, and I still feel about music like I did when I was eighteen." His life might have been turned upside down at the time, but Vince was still Vince— content with his life the way it was, trials and tribulations . . . and all.

TEN

THE KEY

The period from 1997 to 1998 was one of great transition for Vince Gill. Not only was the difficult matter of he and Janis divorcing weighing strongly on his mind, but also his beloved dad, Stan Gill, passed away on July 27, 1997. Vince did the only thing he knew how to do to take his mind off his troubles—he threw himself fully into his career. At the time of Stan's death, Vince was in the midst of a long concert tour with Bryan White, and on some dates they were joined by LeAnn Rimes.

To balance things out, there were several constant things in his life that kept Vince going: his music and the love of his friends, co-workers, and fans. Throughout the year, music industry awards continued to be bestowed upon Gill. When the Nashville Music Awards in 1997 (for 1996) were announced, Vince was declared the Male Vocalist of the Year and their Artist/Songwriter of the Year. At the BMI Songwriter's Awards Gill's "Pretty Little Adriana" and "Go Rest High on That Mountain" were named as being among their Most Performed Songs for the year 1997.

As a concert performer, Vince delivered one of his most satisfying seasons of shows, in spite of the fact that his personal life was in such upheaval. Speaking to the *San Diego Union Tribune* during this phase he said: "Boy! In the old days, you were pretty excited if you had 100 people at your show. Now you expect 9,000 or 10,000. There are a lot of people that are there because they've heard you on the radio. Then there are the others that are still hard-core and fired up about hearing you play a guitar solo and the band play. But I'd say, the majority is there just to hear the hits. I try to satisfy both. . . . And I'm not going to be a big showman with a big, glitzy production. I have to feel I'm being true to myself. . . . The music is definitely first. . . ."

Embarking on his expansive eighty-five city, 1997 concert tour, Vince chose newcomer Bryan White. Young and handsome, Bryan was a perfect opening act for Gill's tour. The young girls would come to swoon over White, and the older-than-eighteen-year-old women would come to cheer on the about-to-be-single Vince.

For anyone who saw Vince in concert during 1997, it was a real treat to hear the *High Lonesome Sound* album brought gleemingly to life. In addition, Bekka Bramlett was often on tour with him, so the songs "Down to New Orleans" and "Tell Me Lover" really sounded as wonderfully alive as they had on record. On stage Gill remained his laid-back, unassuming self. There was no running and jumping around on stage like Garth Brooks, no Las Vegas production numbers and flashy costume changes like Reba McEntire provided, and no sexy dancing à la Shania Twain, and, most of all, *no* cowboy hats.

Most people never consider, or even know of, the existence of the preshow the public never sees: the soundchecks. After the stage is set up, all of the instruments, microphones, lights, amplifiers, mixing board, and speakers are tested by the band and the stars to make certain that everything is in place and working. This is usually done on the afternoon before a show—whether it is in a concert hall or a night club. The test run lasts about ninety minutes with the performers jamming and having fun. The soundchecks were a great opportunity for Vince to blow off steam before the concerts. It also gave him a chance to experiment with new songs and guitar playing styles.

When he invited *Country Music* editor Bob Allen to one of his soundchecks in 1997, Gill said to the writer: "You'll see during soundcheck today that we don't do that many songs that we do in the show. It's a time for everybody in the band to let loose. . . . A couple of songs on this new record, like 'Down to New Orleans' and 'Tell Me Lover,' are just little grooves I figured out up there during soundcheck, and I just stuck them aside 'til I was ready to write songs for the new album."

After his father died, Vince realized that it was time to take a career break. He wasn't certain he could actually do nothing, but for a while he found the proper relax mode gear. "I've never taken a vacation in my whole life," he confessed in an Internet interview on *www.vincegill.com* during this period. "There have been times that a vacation was dictated to me because of lack of success [and] lack of work! It's been pretty odd. I found myself with lots of stuff to do and felt busy some days, and other days had absolutely nothing to do. Sometimes it's great to just spend the day doing nothing."

When his summer tour was over, one of his few appearances in late 1997 came at the International Bluegrass Music Awards show on October 16 at the Center for the Performing Arts in Louisville, Kentucky. Hosting the show was Gill's pal Ricky Skaggs. Vince was on hand as part of the all-star instrumental band, backing up bluegrass pioneer and Bluegrass Hall of Fame member Earl Scruggs. Also in the group were other bluegrass legends, including Kenny Baker, George Shuffler, Rhonda Vincent, Jeff White, and Jeff Guernsey.

Vince's self-imposed sabbatical didn't last for long. He was quick to report in *Country Weekly* magazine by the beginning of 1998: "I'm just getting through a stretch of time that hasn't been the greatest. I've been enjoying staying home at the end of the day. I sit on the couch and go, 'What do I want to do?' Then I think, 'This is kind of neat—nothing!' I haven't been able to do that in a while. But it's awkward, too."

There were so many thoughts racing through his head, that it was inevitable that he should write about his father, his divorce, and his daughter, Jenny, in his new songs. During his planned hiatus, Vince further claimed in *Upbeat* (January 1998) that it was time for still another stylistic change in his music: "I want to make very country sounding records. That's where my head is right now, but nothing is really definite." With so much time on his hands, he couldn't help but turn his mind to his next album.

It wasn't long before Gill began venturing into the recording studio to put some of his new songs on tape. The next thing he knew, he had recorded two full new albums of music. What had been a "vacation" for the star was—in anyone else's terms—a full working period. The tracks he was working on in the country vein eventually became *The Key* (1998).

Although he was on "hiatus," Gill still continued to do charity work at an all-out level. According to him in *Country Weekly* (March 3, 1998): "Ya know, if there's some way I can sing a song or raise some money or help somebody out, it just makes good sense to do it. Even when I first came to Nashville, I invested in the community. I was there to help with anything they needed, as far as charity work or playing and singing on other people's records. It was not just to try and further my career. I was really honest about being everybody's buddy. That's just how I react to life. I mean, I'm the one who has to answer to myself when this is all finished."

In February 1998, Judy Mizell, communications manager of the Grand Ole Opry in Nashville, said in *Country Weekly* magazine: "For three months in a row, Vince has played the Opry almost every weekend."

Indeed, Gill performed there four times in January 1998, compared to seventeen shows in 1997 and twenty-five in 1996. On his first appearance there after the death of his father, he sang "Old Shep" and dedicated it to his dad, who had sung it at home many years ago.

When he debuted the song "The Key to Life," singer/songwriter Bill Anderson wiped tears from his eyes and said from the stage of the Opry, "What a song! What a songwriter! What a singer!"

The next week, his daughter Jenny did "The Key of Life" with him. When they finished, Vince said, "I'm excited about Jenny being here. It's amazing I can get a fifteen-year-old girl out to the Opry on a Saturday night." Obviously, Gill was itching to get back out on the tour road.

When the Grammy Awards were handed out on February 25, 1998, at the Radio City Music Hall in New York City, Vince won his eleventh trophy from the National Academy of Recording Arts & Sciences. The prize he claimed was as the year's Best Country Vocal Performance, Male, for the song "Pretty Little Adriana." This total (of eleven) made him the country performer with the most Grammy Awards in the history of the Grammys to date.

To keep up with his successes at MCA Records, on the concert trail, and at industry award fetes, RCA kept repackaging his material into "hits" albums of their own. In 1997, they had released a ten-cut CD called *Vintage Gill/Encore Collection*. More notable was 1998's *Vince Gill & Friends*. Although only eight cuts in length, this disc under RCA/BMG's Excelsior budget label at least pointed out, song-for-song, on the liner notes who was singing background vocals with him. This offering highlights Vince singing with the likes of Bonnie Raitt, Emmylou Harris, Rodney Crowell, and the Sweethearts of the Rodeo.

On June 12, 1998, Vince was the subject of a CMT cable TV special entitled *Vince Gill: Song & Verse*. As the date approached, he told *Country Weekly* magazine: "The show has no script at all. That's the way I like my life to be. It's amazing to go into a room with someone, create a song, and watch it as it goes into the recording studio and becomes a record. Then a video director listens to the song and turns his perception into a small movie. That's so cool, and that's what this special is going to be about."

As the finality of Vince and Janis's divorce approached, the rumor mill continued to churn. This time the supposed object of Gill's affection was none other than MCA label mate and *Grease* (1978) film star, Olivia Newton-John. The *Globe* tabloid quoted Olivia as gushing about Vince, "I'd marry him in a heartbeat." The same article (June 21, 1998) claimed that one unnamed source had said, "She may be ten years older than him, but they act like a couple of teenagers in love."

On June 16, 1998, MCA Records hosted a concert in Nashville, where Olivia Newton-John performed. When it came time to sing her famed John Travolta duet, "You're the One That I Want," it was Vince who took the stage to sing Travolta's part with Olivia. According to the *Globe*: "He was tenderly holding her hand and hugging and kissing her," during the song. When the label threw a party that evening at the Trace Restaurant, the same publication reported that Olivia and Vince "couldn't take their eyes off each other."

Olivia and Vince had also been seen together in and around Nashville at Planet Hollywood, as well as such nightclubs as the Exit Inn and the Wild Horse. They were also a very visible couple at charity events including a Make-A-Wish outing and the Sara Lee Golf Classic. It sounded at the time like Gill was assuredly the one that Olivia now wanted. Only time would tell if there was any deeper reality to their being together publicly so often.

When Vince and Olivia again sang her *Grease* hit, "You're the One That I Want," at an Operation Smile charity concert in Nashville in 1998, the buzz flew again. According to Vince in *Country Weekly* (March 3, 1998): "[The rumors have been] blown out of proportion. We talked about all kinds of things, but we have no plans for a duet, no plans for a tour, no plans for a lot of things. She's just become a pal and I'm just seeing what transpires."

Gill's divorce from Janis did not become final until June 30, 1998. In the settlement, Janis reportedly kept their $1.75 million, 151-acre horse ranch, as well as the $750,000 home they had shared. In addition, the agreement reportedly stipulated that she would own a percentage of the future songwriting royalties from the songs he penned during their seventeen-year marriage. At the time, however, not all of the settlement terms were made public.

The Gills agreed to share joint custody of their daughter Jenny, who was sixteen years old at the time. Vince also agreed to pay $4,000 per month child support, until Jenny reached the age of eighteen.

In 1998, with his divorce now a reality, Vince was really looking forward to ending his hiatus from the road. He hankered to be back on a tour bus and getting on with his life. "Ahh, the same three chords and the same bus and bunk!" he jokingly said at the time on *www.vincegill.com.* "After twenty-two years it doesn't change a whole lot. All beer joints look alike whether it's an arena, or an old honky-tonk or outdoor pavilion. We're gonna play some different kinds of venues this year, which will be a lot of fun. Just doing what we've always done. . . ." Aside from his family, the most important thing in Gill's life was always his music, and he longed to get back to performing it for his fans, and for himself.

This particular concert trek was put together by CMT—Country Music Television. "I'm really excited about this tour," he announced in *Country Weekly* magazine (June 2, 1998) as it got underway. "Things always have to make sense to me. I'm not very smart. When I heard that CMT was interested in working with me, I thought, 'Well, let's see—they play country music videos twenty-four hours a day and I sing country music and make country music videos. OK, that works.' We're going to go out to about fifty different cities this summer and fall, and I'm really looking forward to getting back out there. I haven't toured in nine months, so I might have forgotten how to play guitar, but I can beat just about anybody in golf."

One of the best aspects of launching this trip was the fact that he was going to be surrounded by his buddies. At different phases of the tour, he had different opening acts. His concert mates in 1998 included Patty Loveless, the reunited group Restless Heart, and newcomer Chely Wright.

Speaking of working with Loveless, Vince told *Upbeat* (January 1998): "I love touring with her. We did about five or six songs together at the end of each show. I would bring her back out and make her sing two or three of her songs and the things she sang with me, 'Go Rest High on That Mountain' and 'When I Call Your Name.' Very few times do voices blend like ours do, unless maybe they're family."

The second act Vince worked with in 1998 were his old friends, the band Restless Heart. The group had six straight number-one hits in the 1980s, including "That Rock Won't Roll," "I'll Still Be Loving You," and "A Tender Lie." Exclaimed Vince in the August 8, 1988, issue of *Country Weekly*: "I missed that camaraderie with those guys, and hearing the dirty jokes and having fun. That whole process is so much a part of who I am that I don't want to slow down."

The group Restless Heart suddenly reunited as a quartet in 1998 and released their *Greatest Hits* album, which included three newly recorded songs. They had previously been a quintet, who had dwindled down to a trio by 1994 when they finally disbanded. Deciding that it was time for a comeback was no easy feat, but they pulled it off with ease, especially with help from their pal Vince. (Years before Gill had been an opening act for Restless Heart.)

Also on several of the 1998 tour dates was singer Chely Wright. Said Vince in that *Country Weekly* article of June 1998: "Chely is someone I thought was really going to make some headway in this industry. She's made a great record and I know she's going to deliver a big hit that will send her career over the top. She's someone to watch. And she plays golf. That was another determining factor for having Chely on the road with me!"

Vince was excited about the array of places at which he would be performing. In turn, audiences anticipated seeing Gill live on stage again.

The great thing about going to a Vince Gill performance is that if he really gets into the show and the audience, he will just play and play, song after song. Not only was the tour overwhelmingly received by the audiences, but the critics loved him too. For example, when he headlined the Universal Amphitheater in Los Angeles on July 10, 1998, writer Darryl Morden (*Hollywood Reporter*) praised: "Gill's performance seemed easy and effortless, marked by skill and craft, but always imbued with heart. . . . Gill can fire up a crowd with nimble fret-dancing fingers like a country [Eric] Clapton, or he can soothe with a plaintive ballad carried by his soaring tenor voice. He's scored his greatest success with ballads, but he skillfully paced this show with an array of rave-ups, shuffles, and rocking numbers as well."

———•◦•◦•———

One of the charity events that Vince participates in yearly is his own celebrity golf tournament. In August 1998, the Sixth Annual Vince Gill Pro-Celebrity Invitational golf tournament was held in Nashville. In his honor, the occasion was dubbed "The Vinny." The celebrity golfers who were on the links with Vince included country stars Glen Campbell, Mark Collie, Charley Pride, Cledus T. Judd, Larry Gatlin, Diamond Rio members Marty Roe and Brian Prout, and rock star Alice Cooper.

According to Gill in the September 1, 1998, issue of *Country Weekly*: "Some people have accused me of loving golf more than music. Actually, I like to combine the two and play as many courses as possible when I'm on tour. And really, some of the best times I've ever had have been with good friends on the golf course. I guess that's why 'The Vinny' is so special to me. I get to play a little golf with my buddies, cut up and have fun, and as a bonus we all get to help out Junior Golf in Tennessee."

That same weekend, the Tennessee Golf Foundation in the town of Franklin dedicated a statue of Vince and his dad, in honor of their support of Junior Golf in the area. "I was pretty tore up," Vince said of the statue's unveiling. Also on hand was Vince's sister Gina, his producer and buddy Tony Brown, and his songwriter friend Guy Clark.

Gill also announced his plans to set up a golf facility for underprivileged children at Shelby Park in Nashville. According to him in a statement to *Country Weekly* (September 1, 1998): "When we started The Vinny . . . I'm not sure any of us imagined that this kind of facility and program would be born from our efforts. I'm proud for all who've done so much to make this possible. It shows what you can accomplish together when you really believe in what you're doing."

There were also several more sports forays to come from Vince in 1998. Of all things for a country singer to do, Gill helped write an article for *Sports Illustrated* magazine. Naturally, it was on the subject of golf and the Pro-Am, as well as the special ambiance of such a tour.

As an indication of how much a sports enthusiast he is, Vince also participated in the start-up of Nashville's new National Hockey League team: the Predators. According to him, in preparation for their first playing season, beginning in October of 1998, he even offered to help sell hockey tickets.

———————

Vince's 1998 road tour was one of the most enjoyable ones he had been on in recent years. He even branched out in his recreational moments. He relaxed on a nearby lake, did a rafting trip, and so forth—in addition, of course, to playing his beloved golf. After the horrendous year he had suffered through in 1997, he was trying hard to make up for lost enjoyment.

———————

The week of August 29, 1998, Vince Gill's seventeenth album, *The Key,* became his first to hit number one on *Billboard*'s Country Albums chart. Not only was it his first album to top the charts, it was also his first to debut at number one!

Explaining the genesis of *The Key,* Gill related that it dated back to the vintage Ray Charles album *Modern Sounds in Country and Western Music.* He explained to the *Los Angeles Daily News* (July 9, 1998): "That's one of my all-time favorite albums. I've loved that record since I was a kid. I've had this idea for a while to do an album like this, but I took the idea to [producer] Tony Brown and told him what a great idea it would be if Michael McDonald did a great soulful country record like Ray Charles did in the '60s. Tony said, 'Well, why don't you do it?' I said, 'Oh, OK.'"

Brown admitted in the same article to being intrigued by the project. "We wanted to cut a country record, plain and simple. Vince's albums have always had a mixture of his traditional side and his contemporary side. The last album really had only one traditional song, 'High Lonesome Sound,' so we decided it was time to stick to Vince's true traditional side. And we usually use Patty Loveless for harmony singing, with Vince singing the third harmony or Billy Thomas singing with him. This time we decided to use all the new young female country artists we could, to give it flavor. And [we] covered all the styles—the shuffles, the ballads. And we wanted to do a song that reminded us of Ray Charles's *Modern Sounds in Country and Western.* That is timeless music."

Vince had an idea in his head, and he wasn't going to be content until he recorded it. As he elaborated for the *Los Angeles Daily News:* "I wanted to bring back the sounds that made country great. . . . Some of my albums have been more fragmented; I tried to make this a whole. I really had a focus of how I wanted to make this record sound."

Not only was this a joyful project to write the music for, but Gill also had a ball selecting the supporting cast of vocalists and musicians. For harmony singers, Vince picked friends to join him, as though he was choosing vocal colors from a paint palette. Among the guest artists utilized were Shelby Lynne, Alison Krauss,

Faith Hill, Lee Ann Womack, Sara Evans, Sonya Isaacs, Curtis Young, Dawn Sears, Billy Thomas, and Jeff White. Vince also sings the duet, "My Kind of Woman/My Kind of Man" with Patty Loveless. The musicians he chose included Randy Scruggs and veteran piano player Hargus "Pig" Robbins.

Vince stitched the album together with a mix of older songs he had composed nearly a dozen years ago and some newer songs that he created specifically for the album. It was recorded from December 1997 through February 1998.

He had certain sounds in mind, and, instead of hiring new players to mimic the sound of the music from the early 1960s, he simply found the original players. He outlined in *Country Weekly* in mid-August 1998: "I hired Pig Robbins, who played on all those great Patsy Cline records and other great records in the '50s and '60s. Steve Gibson, who played in Jerry Reed's band, can do anything. He is really a great chameleon. I could go to him and say, 'Do you remember when this guy played on this record?' and he could recreate the whole sound. Randy Scruggs played all the acoustic parts. Glenn Worf played bass. Every note counts on these records, and every person's contribution counts. It's a combination of people's hearts, souls, and sounds. That's why I enjoy the record making process as much as anything. Music is not about hoarding for yourself. The joy is letting people discover other people's talents."

"This one is country from top to bottom," Vince said of *The Key* in his 1998 MCA press biography. "There are a lot of left-field country records out there, and I've certainly made my share of them. But lately I've found myself just missing real, true country music. . . . I knew I wanted to write a very traditional record. I knew the kinds of songs that needed to be written. So I just decided to buckle down and do it."

Although the musicianship that went into the album, *The Key,* is undeniable, it is an album that is not overstuffed with joy.

The topics, the issues, and the emotions that are contained on this release are often a "downer." The excitement that was brimming over in *High Lonesome Sound* was not evident on *The Key*. Ultimately, this might have hurt sales of this album.

The Key opens on a high note with the light and peppy "Don't Come Crying to Me," which was written by Vince Gill and Reed Nielson. With his voice blending beautifully with Dawn Sears, this is a wonderful bit of nuevo-nostalgia set to a shuffle beat. According to Vince at a May 1998 press conference: "I've [only] recorded a couple of shuffles. When I [do], it's like I'm hearing Ray Price, Webb Pierce, or Faron Young. There's an upright bass, fiddle, steel, and they all play the signature melody and the bass walks and it's big, fat, and sweet. The harmony vocal goes straight tenor to fifth above, back and forth. What I've always tried to do is respect and honor what's real. I don't try to water it down. You don't hip up a shuffle!"

Immediately slowing things down, the intriguing "If You Ever Have Forever in Mind," which Gill collaborated on with Troy Seals, is a classic ballad of infatuation. It even has a 1950s style background choir, the kind who might accompany Patti Page back then. "I think this is my tip-of-the-hat to the classic Nashville Sound," explained Gill in his press biography. "Remember those Ray Charles records where he was doing 'Born to Lose' and 'Crying Time' and all those? That's what I wanted this to sound like."

"I Never Really Knew You 'Til You Said Goodbye," which Gill penned, mirrors the end of his marriage. It is hard to separate this tongue-in-cheek medium-paced little ditty about love lost from the demise of his long relationship with Janis.

Vince's composition "Kindly Keep It Country" echoes the statements that the singing star has made about his return to a 100 percent country sound. "That song has been in my brain my whole life basically. When I was in Pure Prairie League we used to sit around and pretend we had this fictitious radio station called KKIC. We'd pretend we were disc jockeys and announce, 'KKIC, Kindly Keep It Country.' That just stuck with me." The voice that accompanies Vince so beautifully on this song is Lee Ann Womack.

"All Those Years" by Vince is about someone who has just been dumped by his wife and is inviting a date over to console him. With lines that in essence say 'Pardon me if I call her name out in the middle of the evening,' it isn't hard to imagine where the inspiration came for this one. One of the most interesting aspects of "All Those Years" is the fact that Vince uses a lower vocal register than his fans are used to hearing. It was another way of stretching his performance.

"I'll Take Texas" is a fun up-beat change of pace, singing the praises of the Lone Star State, and Gill is joined by Shelby Lynne in this sure-fire moonlight and campfire ode. "This song is Bob Wills; it's western swing," Vince said in his 1998 record label biography. "This kind of music was all around me growing up. My area, the whole Oklahoma/Texas tradition is all about those dance halls. The lesson here is that music doesn't have to rock real hard to feel real good."

One of the true highlights on this album is Vince's duet with Patty Loveless. It was so popular that it was even nominated for a Grammy Award. According to Gill at his spring 1998 press conference: "The song's called 'You're My Kind of Woman/You're My Kind of Man.' It's a match made in heaven by God's gentle hands. And it's neat because it's not just someone singing harmony on a record and saying it's a duet. . . . It's very reminiscent of Conway [Twitty] and Loretta [Lynn], steel [guitar], fiddles, and strings."

Vince's "There's Not Much Love Here Anymore," is slow and sad, sad, sad. It is a true crying song. "I try to keep [the divorce] as private as possible in terms of what I say in interviews and such . . . out of respect for everybody involved. But there is a lot of me in that song," he admits. "I was really doing that. I was sitting in the house, the rain was pouring down, and I was not the happiest camper in town," he told the *Los Angeles Times* (August 1998).

Although lively in tempo, "Let Her In" is another sad song, in which the singer is asking his daughter to accept his new lady friend, now that his wife has gone. Hmmmm? Who could this possibly be about? However, Vince claimed in the *Los Angeles Times* (August 2, 1998): "That's an interesting one to bring up, because the song's really not about me. I've got a buddy who has three kids from a previous marriage. He was getting ready to remarry. One of the kids was really struggling with it. That's something a lot of people are going through these days."

"Hills of Carolina" is another morose composition. Instead of sounding like 1950s country, it is more like an 1850s tune about loving the slopes of Carolina and wanting to be buried in them when he dies. Not exactly a cheerful theme.

Although "Live to Tell It All" is a slow-paced waltz, it is beautifully sung by Vince, with Sonya Isaacs (with whom he co-wrote the song) behind him, and is a refreshing departure on this album. That is to say that it is one of the few cuts on *The Key* where no one dies, gets left behind, is heartbroken, or is picking out a grave. (Isaacs toured with Gill in 1998 and for her debut on a new label, Lyric Street Records, Vince planned to produce the album.)

Another song of devotion, "What They All Call Love," is sung wonderfully with Faith Hill. The saddest song of all is saved for last, however, as Vince sings of the death of his beloved father. "The Key to Life," although up-tempo, is a two-tissue affair. Even sadder is the fact that the music played on the number comes from Stan Gill's own instrument. As Gill emotionally explained to the *Los Angeles Daily News* (July 9, 1998); "So, I play his old banjo on that song. He wasn't a great player, but he had a kind of rhythm sound to his playing, and you can hear that on there." The song meant a lot to Vince: "'The Key to Life' . . . it may be my favorite song I've ever written. It's about my papa and everything he taught me. He really was a good man. He was a lawyer and a judge. I learned early what was good," he told *Country Weekly* in June 1998.

Vince admitted that he had been a bit scalded by his fans who shied away from his *High Lonesome Sound* album. "I got my hand slapped on the last record in that I tried to explain [up front] what it was, and what I was attempting to do. In the explanation, it gets blown out of proportion and a lot of people thought *High Lonesome Sound* was a bluegrass album, he reported on the Web site *www.vincegill.com*.

Although wonderfully played and exquisitely crafted, it is hard not to think of *The Key* as Vince Gill's "death and divorce" album. He admitted in a 1998 press conference: "I think most people are going to look at what's transpired over the last bit of time, and make that conclusion regardless of what the songs may or may not mean. So in spots, 'yes,' but in spots, 'no.' Once again, I think people will take what they see going in and gravitate towards it. The most poignant song to me is about my father and it's called 'Key of Life.' That one's pretty special. Some of the rest are too, but that one's really the heart on the sleeve."

Perhaps, more than anything else, recording the album *The Key* was a catharsis. Vince seemingly cared little whether it was commercial. It was the music that he felt like making at that given time. "What was really a joy about making this record is knowing that I'd didn't want to do any song with a rock groove or a pop groove," he insisted. "I wanted to make a record that was as country at the start as it is at the end. . . . For a long period of time, nobody wanted to hear a steel guitar, because it defined a song as country. It kind of got to a point where nobody played those crying, really weepy, kind of solos," he set forth to *Country Weekly* (August 18, 1998).

Of his writing on *The Key,* Gill explained in the June 2, 1998, edition of *Country Weekly:* "The last record I made inspired me to write some songs by myself again. Something that we do a lot of in Nashville is co-writing. But on the last record I wrote alone a lot—just as an exercise to see if I could, with some discipline, finish a song myself. Plus, with all the things that went on in my life last year [1997], I wanted to be the one to make the statements that I made with these songs and wrote what was in here. . . . I don't want the songwriting community to think I'll always write my own songs, but I think if you want to be a truly great songwriter, your goal should be to write and record your own songs."

In September 1998, Vince was slated to host the Country Music Association's annual awards. Now, with forty-two nominations to his name, Vince is close to tying his idol Merle Haggard—who has forty-four—for most nominations ever. With regard to that honor, Vince said at the time in the September 1, 1998, issue of *Country Weekly:* "There's no way anyone can compare me with Hag. He's one of the guys that taught me how to do what I do. There's no way that if I ever sell more records or get more nominations it means I'm a better artist. That's just silly."

For the Country Music Association Awards on CBS-TV in September 1998, Gill was nominated as Entertainer of the Year, alongside Brooks & Dunn, Garth Brooks, Tim McGraw, and George Strait. Said Vince in the September 21, 1998, issue of *Country Weekly;* "I stay pretty grounded and realize I don't do what I do to win awards. I feel like I'm fortunate and lucky, but I've worked hard, and you know, you create your good luck with hard work. It's interesting about the awards. If it was about who was the biggest, baddest record-seller of all, then we wouldn't need to vote. We could all just go, 'Okay, you win, you win, and you win.' But that ain't the way it works."

On September 15, 1998, Vince appeared on the CBS-TV show *Late Night with David Letterman*. Also on the program was popular Asian actor and martial arts expert, Jackie Chan. Chan was in New York City promoting his new book, and Gill was on the talk show to sing his latest hit single, "If You Ever Have Forever on Your Mind," and to discuss the upcoming CMA Awards telecast.

Through the talkfest, amusingly cynical Letterman quipped one-liners starting with the phrase, "If I had a voice like Vince Gill . . ." It was a great plug for Vince, even though the host beat the joke into the ground by the time Vince—the evening's final guest—arrived on camera.

When Gill finally took the stage, it was to sing his hit, "Forever." Joining David at the podium for a brief dialogue before the end credits rolled, he and Letterman laughed about their ability to host awards shows on the CBS network. When David asked Vince how it felt to be the follow-up act to a martial arts expert (that is Jackie Chan) doing an Elvis Presley impersonation, Gill didn't miss a beat, laughingly exclaiming, "Jackie Chan stole my show!"

On September 23, 1998, the thirty-second annual Country Music Association Awards was broadcast from the Grand Ole Opry stage in Nashville. Among the notables on the program were Trace Adkins, LeAnn Rimes, George Strait, the Dixie Chicks, Brooks & Dunn, Garth Brooks, Faith Hill, Alan Jackson, Patty Loveless, Kathy Mattea, Reba McEntire, Randy Scruggs, Travis Tritt, Wynonna Judd, and Trisha Yearwood.

Not only did Vince host the proceedings, but he opened the program with Randy Scruggs doing the instrumental they had recorded together for Scruggs's album *Crown of Jewels* (Warner Bros., 1998)—"A Soldier's Joy." As usual, Gill made a very natural and relaxed emcee of the fast-paced three-hour show. Along the way he tossed off Monica Lewinsky jokes, poked fun at the volume of Shania Twain's production number, and acted silly with the Dixie Chicks. He also made jokes about his weight. Although not overweight, he had put on a few pounds in the past two years, but at least he had a sense of humor about it.

Vince kept the proceedings moving while awards were handed out, and tributes to several singers and songwriters were presented by a galaxy of Nashville stars. In the category of Male Vocalist of the Year, the nominees included Garth Brooks, Tim McGraw, Collin Raye, George Strait, and Vince Gill. The winner was George Strait.

The most touching moment of the evening came when Vince performed "The Key to Life," which he played on his father's guitar. While he sang, he became audibly choked with emotion. In fact, his voice cracked several times during the performance, and he was near tears by the song's end.

The nominees for Entertainer of the Year were Garth Brooks, George Strait, Brooks & Dunn, Tim McGraw, and Vince Gill. Kris Kristofferson presented the trophy, which went to Garth. When Kris announced Garth's win, Brooks was shown accepting the award in Buffalo where he then was appearing in concert. In Nashville, Vince returned to center stage and yelled teasingly, "Must be present to win! Must be present to win!" Although Gill didn't go home with any prizes that night—for the first time in ages—he was great as the undisputed star of the evening, masterfully playing emcee to the festivities.

Vince continued to participate on several other albums during 1998. One of these occasions was to produce a song by Patty Loveless for the album *A Tribute to Tradition* (Sony). As Loveless explained it in *Country Weekly* (June 2, 1998): "Vince and I got to work together recently, when I asked him to produce a traditional song of Loretta Lynn's I recorded, called 'Wine, Women, and Song.' He did a great job. He knows I'm in there kicking myself all over the place, and it feels good to know he gives me the freedom to do what I need to do. I trust him."

In time for the 1998 holiday season, Vince was one of the country music stars to contribute to the DreamWorks album *The Prince of Egypt—Nashville*. An interesting concept disc tied into the then current animated feature film *The Prince of Egypt*, it was a potpourri of songs used in the movie, including "If You Believe," the duet by Whitney Houston and Mariah Carey, which was nominated for—and won—an Academy Award. For this release, however, the same story, the Bible story of Moses in Egypt, is told by several country singers, either using the music from the film or writing their own. Pam Tillis sings her composition "Milk and Honey," Reba McEntire does, "Please Be the One," and Vince Gill contributes "Once in Awhile," which he wrote with Reed Nielsen. For the recording, Vince is heard with vocal accompaniment by Michael McDonald and Tabitha Fair. Having Michael on this album made this inspirational ballad a case of Pure Prairie League meets the Doobie Brothers!

Vince was also heard on the aforementioned Randy Scruggs's album, *Crown of Jewels*. Gill is on the song "A Soldier's Joy," an instrumental track, which starts off the disc. Also on the record are other friends of Scruggs such as Bruce Hornsby, Trisha Yearwood, Mary Chapin Carpenter, John Prine, and Rosanne Cash. Scruggs is well-known in Nashville for being the producer of the 1989 album *Will the Circle Be Unbroken, Vol. 2,* which was done with the Nitty Gritty Dirt Band and an all-star cast as well.

In addition, the ever busy Gill released his eighteenth album, and his second one with a Christmas motif, *Breath of Heaven*. When asked if he had written any new holiday songs for the outing, Vince laughed at the idea. "Absolutely not!" he said in his spring 1998 press conference. "I remember about five years ago, the first Christmas record, I sat down with my guitar and went 'Mistletoe . . . Tree . . . Oh, never mind, let's go find the classics. . . .' [This is] my opportunity to step out of my country career, so to speak, and try to be a Nat King Cole or a Frank Sinatra. . . ."

In addition to preparing and releasing *Breath of Heaven,* and letting it promote itself, Gill did a short all-Christmas music series of concert performances. Plotting it out in the beginning of 1998, he projected: "It'll be fun to do a Christmas Tour because I can do a complete night of Christmas music, now that I've got two albums to do. Last year, or year before last, we did half the show acoustically with a few of the hits, then put on the tuxedos and did Christmas songs."

The songs Gill included on his second Christmas album were mainly traditional choices, including "Winter Wonderland," "O Little Town of Bethlehem," "Silver Bells," "Blue Christmas," and "Let It Snow, Let It Snow, Let It Snow." Amy Grant was one of the few writers to contribute something new for the release. As Gill explained it in *Country Weekly* (December 1, 1998): "The first time Amy and I did a Christmas show together in Nashville about five years ago, I heard Amy sing 'Breath of Heaven.' I thought it was so beautiful. The next year Amy asked me what I wanted to sing, and I told her I wanted to sing 'Breath of Heaven.' She said, 'You can't.' I said, 'Why not?' And Amy said, 'Because it's the story of Mary. You'd sound goofy singing it.' I guess I didn't hear all the words. When it came time to do this record, I thought maybe I could do the song from the perspective of Joseph, and maybe those words could be interpreted by a man. So I called Amy and asked her if she could change a word or two so I could sing the song. I think it translates well, and it turned out real special."

The *Breath of Heaven* disc was a big hit and took Vince in a totally different musical direction. Instead of hiring country musicians to do the typical Nashville holiday album, Gill had composer/arranger Patrick Williams conduct a complete orchestra behind him. Suddenly, Vince was recording a whole album in a Frank Sinatra mode.

Although he is stylistically all over the boards with his albums, all of Vince Gill's productions have several unifying themes: quality music, meticulous instrumentation, insightful lyrics, and that incredible voice of his. Whether it was 1950s–1960s country music, orchestrated pop music, or inspiring film music, Vince Gill continued his own career tradition of making the kind of music that pleases him, regardless of the commercial aspects that so often get in the way of true artists.

ELEVEN

VINCE ON VINCE

As one of the most well-respected singer/songwriters in twentieth-century country music, Vince Gill has not only won more awards than most performers ever dream of, and has attained the kind of stature that most people only hope to attain, the world still wants to know more and more about the man behind the music. Although he is a very private person, his life is pretty much an open book.

With all that the public knows about him, his life, and his creativity, more and more unanswered questions come to mind. For instance, with all of the great music coming out Nashville, and surely the pick of the crop at his fingertips, why doesn't Vince do cover versions of well-known tunes on his albums. According to him in *Upbeat* magazine in 1998: "It's very hard to say because as a writer, I really do like to create songs. I guess 'I Fall to Pieces' would be one of my favorites. I can remember as a kid we had Patsy Cline records going at home all the time. I really learned about her through my parents."

How much of Vince's song subject matter is autobiographical, and how much is fabricated? He declines to answer that one, saying only that, "The neat thing about writing songs is you can tell the truth or lie your face off—like my golf score," as he informed the *Hollywood Reporter* in July 1998.

What is his least favorite part about being a 1990s music star? According to Gill it is shooting music videos: "In all honesty, I wish I didn't have to do a video. Everybody that reads this is going to say, 'Why did he say that? That idiot!' I never like to look at music. I like to hear music. In our day and age, it's become a very visually painted society. I always saw what I heard. Now people hear what they see. There's a big difference there," he set forth to *Upbeat* magazine in an extended article for its January 1998 issue.

Is there a strategy for him releasing his singles? As he elaborated for *Upbeat:* "I find it real hard to be real creative every twelve months. I feel like if you make a great album full of great songs, you can go to that well for a long time for singles and hits. . . . I never want to record a new record until they'd released everything I'd hope they would off of the current record. I feel like, if the water is running and it feels good, don't turn it off."

As for his favorite sport, how much does he really love golf? Well, so much that he will gladly caddy for his buddies, if there is a tournament he really wants to observe up close. To prove the point, Gill refers to the time his pal Bob Wolcott (who plays in the Nike tour) was seeking to qualify for the U.S. Open in Columbus, Ohio. Vince caddied the thirty-six-hole event for his pal, even when it started to rain. For Gill, it was a blast to be in the proximity of all the athletes he usually only watched on TV playing the green.

Now that he is such a big star in Nashville, will he continue to do so many guest appearances on his friends' albums? The answer is yes, according to Vince in that same *Upbeat* article. He thrives on being part of the recording process no matter what his particular role on a project might be. "I go back to that same thing about when you make records. It's not all about the star sitting up there on a pedestal and everything around him or her doesn't mean anything or isn't as important. That's just not true. I've always said that

Don Rich was as important to the sound of Buck Owens as Buck Owens. The same goes for the guitar playing of James Burton and Elvis Presley. There are reasons why songs are hits, and there are reasons why people love those songs." It is just this humility that has endeared Vince to so many members of the industry.

If Vince himself were going to define "the Vince Gill style," what would it be? "He doesn't have one; he's a chameleon," the singer aptly assessed for the Summer 1995 issue of *Country Guitar*. "And you know, I think I like that better! I like being able to pick the Tele [-caster guitar] and play like Albert [Lee] and James [Burton] in a sense, but with my own little quirks. But it's also a blast to be able to pick up another guitar and be a totally different kind of player, . . . My playing is an extension of my singing. If I'm out there singing an R&B tune, I wouldn't want to sing it with a little bit of the nasal twang. That wouldn't be true to the style."

On his albums, how does he lay down his guitar parts? Vince detailed to *Country Guitar:* "There are no set ways I lay parts down. For example, if I have a riff that might kick off the song or become a signature part, I'll lay it down first. A good example of that is the intro riff to 'One More Last Chance.' The whole song completely fell into place after the lick was established. Other times, I'll come in at the end, after all the basics have been recorded, and lay down fills and solos—whatever I feel work. It's always fun, because Steuart Smith and Randy Scruggs, the other guitar players on my last few albums, are well aware that I want to play, so they always leave me plenty of space for my parts."

With all of the recordings he has appeared on to date, how does he keep it fresh song after song? "I like to let the other musicians have a big part in creating the parts. . . . I think that sometimes you diminish your results when you tell everyone what to play. . . . Sometimes more heads are better than one. I'm fairly hands-on in the studio, but not enough to get in the way."

Who is Vince Gill? A musician, or a star? According to him in *Country Guitar:* "For years, I was known for being a good player and singer, but only within the circles of the music industry and the musicians themselves. I always played in the 'musician's musician' bands. Now, I'm on the other side. So in a way, it's refreshing that after a show, people will come up to me and say, 'We always knew you could sing, but we had no idea you could play the guitar.' And my current band is made up of monster players, so playing is as fun as ever."

How did Vince end up with the title in Nashville as "Mr. Nice Guy"? He claimed in *New Country* in 1996: "It's not put on, not something that I attempted to do. . . . I'm just the way I am." He also admits, "It's kinda sad to me that it shocks people that I'm nice. They say, 'You're so nice and normal and down-to-earth,' and it's like 'Well, what did you expect?' I just try to be decent to people, that's all."

Does fame constrain him? "I go everywhere," he told *New Country* in June 1997. "I'm never gonna hide from any of this. I like being a part of the world too much to seclude myself. Fans know I'm extremely approachable, and if they get all giddy I just laugh at 'em. Sometimes I laugh about how I'm always walking up to somebody that feels like they're gonna say somethin' to me, like, 'I liked your hair better short,' or 'I liked your hair better long,' or 'You look tired'—you know, just on and on. And I think, 'You know, I don't feel compelled to walk up to you and say, "Where did you get that dress, that's hideous!" ' But, that's okay, I don't mind. It's certainly not meant with any malice. You know what it is? I think people like to trust things. They like to trust that I'm gonna look like I look to them, and that I'm gonna sing like I normally sing. You know, I put trust in this Wendy's hamburger, that it's gonna taste like the Wendy's hamburger I had the other day, you know?"

What is his technique in picking voices for his albums? If someone sings with him, does that mean he will return the favor? Said Gill in a mid-1998 press conference for the Radio Syndicated

Round Table: "Well, I don't think I've ever operated on the theory that if you sing on my record, I'll sing on yours. It's never been about that. I did it for a living. I was a session musician—I played and sang on everybody's records and I got called to do a lot of that because that's what I have the talent to do, not because I became famous as a singer. It's not name value. I can guarantee you that I've never looked at it from that perspective. . . . I try to cast voices I hear in my head. Not famous voices, just voices."

How does he see his position in country music today? "I think all I can do is what moves me," he put forth at a mid-1998 press conference. "I'm not out to be the new Roy Acuff or save the Opry and make a traditional record and say, 'Hey, everybody: We're going too far!' That's not what I'm doing. 'Cause I've enjoyed the success of making a record like 'Don't Let Our Love Start Slipping Away,' and there's nothing about that record that's country! But the parameters are not what they were in 1940, 1950, '60, '70 or '80. They're parameters of today and you just love and record within them. I'm fortunate I can step outside those bounds a little and make a record like *High Lonesome Sound*. Some of those songs would never be played on country radio and I knew that. But once again, I'm not out to say this is the definition of how you should think, and this is not the definition of music as you should hear it. It's strictly me. It's what I love. . . ."

Where does he feel that country music is heading? "Well, I think if you go back and listen to what I said, or a lot of people said five years ago, it was hey, everybody be careful." According to Vince in a media round table in 1998, "Everybody's going to jump on the bandwagon and you're going to rely on the youth, and they're going to go away. That demographic has never been a part of country music until maybe the last ten years. And now it has been, and you see it's not something [you can count on]—I'm not going to hang my hat on a seventeen-year-old kid and have them be the focal point for my future."

Does he find that different recording studios have different sound quality? "We did a bunch of stuff in the Sound Emporium [in Nashville] for this new record [*The Key*], an older studio with an older vibe. [It's] those shingles on the roof!" he claimed in that same press conference. "Some of the newer studios are more clinical—definite vibes. The rooms sound different. You can build a studio, put all the same gear in it, design it the same way, and it still sounds different. We recorded in a new studio called Ocean Way in the old Tony Alamo Church here in Nashville. They all have characteristics. What was neat about being in the Sound Emporium was the strings sounded rich. And the bottom end at Ocean Way had so much more depth. Sometimes you know you're in a place that has a lot of history, like the old RCA studio here in Nashville. A lot of great records were made there. It's like going to play golf on a course you've seen on TV. It makes for a good spirit."

Does he personally feel connected with Music City? According to him in *Country Weekly* magazine in mid-1997: "I just like being part of the community. I haven't tried to do all the things I've done to try to be a kingpin in the city of Nashville. I'm just trying to help the community I live in. It just makes sense. It's where you live, and if you make this place better, you make it better for yourself, as well."

If he had one piece of advice to give those starting out in the music business, what would that be? According to a recent interview posted on the Internet at *www.vincegill.com,* he answered: "Be patient! There's no rules, you know. Some people come to town and get the break right away and other people come and struggle and struggle. What works for one doesn't work for the next one. I came here and kind of struggled for seven years, but at the same time it didn't feel like a struggle to me. It felt like progress. If you believe, I say you need to come here and embrace this town if you want to be part of it. It's certainly not going to come and get you."

And that brings us to the conclusion of this edition of: *The World According to Gill.*

TWELVE

THE HEART WON'T LIE

After eighteen album releases, five number-one hit singles, and more trophies than he can count, Vince Gill has *just started* creating music. According to him, he is in for the long haul when it comes to musical creativity. He could certainly fill several CDs with all of the featured songs he has done on movie soundtracks, tribute albums, and guest appearances on others' releases.

With *High Lonesome Sound*'s cajun flavoring, with *The Key*'s country stylings, with *Breath of Heaven*'s orchestrated pop sound, or with the rock 'n' roll he has demonstrated singing with Little Feat and with Pure Prairie League, the door is open for all sorts of future recording possibilities.

One of the projects that has been bantered about is Vince either doing, or headlining, a tribute album utilizing the songs of the late John Denver, another famous singing star who walked the line between country music and pop/rock. "That would be a great idea," said Gill not long ago on *www.vincegill.com.* "Unfortunately, things just don't always work even when you want to do something. . . . I'd like to do an instrumental album someday. I'd like to do a total bluegrass album, and all the above. Unfortunately, you're not going to get it all done in a lifetime, so I do my best, and do what I know I need to do."

And, what about that long talked about duet album with Patty Loveless? Will that ever see the light of day? It certainly didn't hurt that their duet from *The Key*, "My Kind of Woman/My Kind of Man," was nominated for a Grammy Award in 1998. Pondered Vince in a press conference: "A whole album? I don't know. Could be. We recorded a song on this record that I've always envisioned as a flagship song for that possibility and it still could happen. It would be neat, but the way things work today, it's very difficult to get all those schedules in order. It's very difficult to find the perfect time."

Whatever career direction he plans to go in next, Vince is apparently content to just let the chips fall where they will. His album sales aren't of much concern to him, so long as he is satisfied creatively with what he is doing. He has a very strong fan base, but he knows that admirers are fickle and that popularity comes and goes. Of his fans he told *Country Weekly* (August 18, 1998): "I'm not afraid of when they're going to go, 'Click! Next!' Because it's going to happen. To deny that it's going to happen is foolish. Maybe I'll be one of the lucky ones like George Strait who has real longevity. And I think that's because I haven't always tried to make a record that fit the mold for that week. I've tried to consistently record good songs. The good songs will still always win."

Recently, followers of Vince's, who had met through his Web site on the Internet, raised $10,000 in memory of Vince's father at St. Jude's Hospital. Gill was blown away by that gesture. "Well, I'm obviously extremely flattered that the people care," said Gill on *www.vincegill.com* some months ago. "I don't have a computer and I wouldn't know how to turn one on, so in all honesty, this is very foreign to me, but all very sweet. The fact that they not only care about my music but the things in my life is very comforting. It helps more than they probably ever will understand and is appreciated more than I can tell them because I'm not going to learn how to type!"

If his current hot streak continues: *magnifique!* If it all falls apart: *c'est la vie!*

One of his main concerns at the moment is raising his daughter, Jenny. During a syndicated radio roundtable interview in the spring of 1998, he was asked whether it made him nervous that teenaged Jenny was now driving. Said proud father Vince in that same interview, "No. She's a good driver. I took her driving with me all the time when she had her permit. She's done real good so far."

Watching both her father and her mother juggle musical careers throughout her life, Jenny Gill has now gotten the music bug herself. There are certainly a lot of teenagers her age on the musical charts: from LeAnn Rimes to the Wilkinsons. According to Gill in the August 18, 1998, edition of *Country Weekly*: "She's got a couple of bands that she's playing in and loves it, and they're actually playing out at some coffeehouses and getting some gigs here and there, and I love to go. She doesn't have any idea how neat it feels to me to watch her up there doing what she does." Vince was quite worried that Jenny would launch a singing career before she was mature enough to handle it. Per protective daddy, "I've basically said, 'You're not going to get to do any of this stuff until you're a little more grown-up,' because I do want her to be a kid. That's the greatest time of life, you know, and so she knows that she has to be a kid for a while."

He is, however, very supportive of all of her ventures. For example, he became involved in raising funds for Jenny's cheerleading squad. In addition, he addressed some of the students at her school as part of "The Grammy in the Schools" program, to teach youngsters about music education.

At the end of 1998, Vince's name was prominently displayed when publications tallied their annual "End of the Year" lists of the best and worst albums. In the December 29, 1998, issue of *USA Today*, critic

Brian Mansfield listed Vince's song "If You Ever Have Forever in Mind" number three on his Top Ten singles. The list included: 1) "You're Still the One" by Shania Twain, 2) "This Kiss" by Faith Hill, 3) "If You Ever Have Forever in Mind," 4) "I Said a Prayer" by Pam Tillis, 5) "Dance the Night Away" by the Mavericks, 6) "There's Your Trouble" by the Dixie Chicks, 7) "Holes in the Floor of Heaven" by Steve Wariner, 8) "Bye, Bye" by Jo Dee Messina, 9) "Powerful Thing" by Trisha Yearwood, and 10) "Wide Open Spaces" by the Dixie Chicks.

In that same issue of *USA Today*, Vince's album, *The Key*, was heralded as the number-one country album of the year. Claimed journalist Brian Mansfield: "While country wrestled with its roots, Vince Gill embraced his, from bluegrass to lavish Ray Charles–inspired country-pop." The albums which followed Gill's included: 2) *Some Things I Know* by Lee Ann Womack, 3) *Teatro* by Willie Nelson, 4) *High Mileage* by Alan Jackson, 5) *Wide Open Spaces* by the Dixie Chicks, 6) *Hungry Again* by Dolly Parton, 7) *Closer to the Fire* by Waylon Jennings, 8) *Trampoline* by the Mavericks, 9) *Where Your Road Leads* by Trisha Yearwood, and 10) *One Step at a Time* by George Strait.

The year 1998 had been a strong year for country music in general. There were more country-formatted radio stations in the United States that year than any other genre of music, including rock and pop. Also, country album sales were up from 1997, according to *Billboard* magazine. In their year-end issue, reporter Chet Flippo likewise named *The Key* on his critical list of Top Ten country albums of 1998.

Vince began 1999 in full form, by starring in the A&E hour-long cable TV Special, *By Request Only*. Sitting in a New York City recording studio, Gill literally played his hits on command in this unique media presentation.

On February 25, 1999, he was set to perform his hit song "If You Ever Have Forever in Mind," at the Shrine Auditorium in Los Angeles. That afternoon, in a non-broadcast segment, he and Randy Scruggs had won a Grammy Award in the category of Best Country Instrumental for the song "A Soldier's Joy" on Randy's album. This was Grammy number twelve for Vince.

Also on the telecast that evening was Madonna, wearing a bizarre red kabuki outfit, Shania Twain in thigh-high boots and hot pants, and Ricky Martin exploding forth on stage in a carnival of excitement. Amid this setting was Vince, with his lushly orchestrated ballad "If You Ever Have Forever in Mind," complete with a string section. It was a classy musical moment that was broadcast to countless millions of homes around the world. He then proceeded to win his thirteenth Grammy Award, when that same song was named the 1998 Best Country Vocal Performance, Male, by the National Academy of Recording Arts & Sciences. His song had overcome stiff competition, including "Nothing But the Taillights" by Clint Black, "To Make You Feel My Love" by Garth Brooks, and "Holes in the Floor of Heaven" by Steve Wariner.

In addition to all of the attention his recording career was continuing to receive, Gill was also big news in the tabloids. In early 1999, when Amy Grant suddenly filed for divorce from her husband, Gary Chapman (who is the host of the television program, *Prime Time Country*), it was widely speculated in the press that the reason for her action was to become available to marry Vince. The media coverage ranged from tastefully tongue-in-cheek, as in "Baby Baby Goodbye" in *People* magazine (January 18, 1999), to highly impolite, as headlined in "Amy Grant Dumps Hubby and She's Free for Vince Gill" for the *Globe* (January 18, 1999), and in *Star*'s proclamation (January 26, 1999) that "Vince Gill Stole My

Wife. . . . Amy Grant's Bitter Hubby Reveals Real Reason Behind Bust-Up."

Country America magazine in January 1999 brought forth new details in the divorce settlement of the Gills. According to this publication, Janis was to receive 38 percent of all of Vince's earnings from the songs he wrote and recorded from the beginning of his career through 1997 when they divorced. Since his time with Pure Prairie League, Vince always published his music under the name of Benefit Music. Those are the songs in which Janis now owns a percentage. Starting anew, and beginning with 1998's *The Key* album, Vince now publishes his music through Vinnie Mae Music in which Janis is *not* involved.

It was also revealed that, at the time of Vince and Janis's split-up, he was worth approximately $20 million. In their settlement, Janis reportedly received $6 million in cash, plus the earlier-mentioned 150-acre farm, located south of Nashville—valued at one-and-a-half million dollars, and their $700,000 house. Janis also kept ownership of the dress shop that she and her sister opened in Franklin.

In a dramatic article in the *Star* newspaper (June 22, 1999), entitled "I Fled in Terror from Raging Vince Gill," divorce court transcripts outlined some of Janis and Vince's marital disputes. The most heated one had Janis alleging "[Vince] lost control of his temper and picked up a chair with the intention of throwing it out the window of my home." Although the claim could be interpreted as extreme *furniture abuse*, it sounded more like a normal but heated marital dispute and not nearly as threatening as the enticing headline would lead one to believe.

Throughout 1999, the speculation about Vince's personal life continued to simmer. Reporters linked Amy Grant's ex-husband Gary Chapman with movie star Ashley Judd. Ashley had appeared on his TV show with her famous singing mother and sister—Naomi and Wynonna Judd, and Ashley and Gary instantly hit it off. In an article in the April 30, 1999, issue of *Star* tagged "Ashley Judd in Hot New Romance with Amy Grant's Ex," someone named as "a source" claimed, "Most people think that when the dust settles from the breakup, Amy will wind up with Vince Gill."

The October 5, 1999, issue of *Star* ran a story headlined "WHO'S THE BLONDE? Amy Grant Travels in Disguise with Vince Gill." Apparently, unable to tolerate being apart, Amy had taken to disguising herself with blonde wigs and stowing away on Gill's tour bus during several play dates of his 1999 concert tour. In a related story in that same issue, it was revealed that Amy Grant and Gary Chapman's divorce had become final on June 17, 1999. Their $30 million divorce was swiftly resolved, with a fair division of property and possessions, and joint custody of their three children.

During this high visibility period, neither Vince nor Amy made any statements to either confirm or deny any of the swirling rumors as to the extent of their relationship. Gossip columnists had a field day speculating as to what their future plans would be, and whether or not they'd be announcing wedding plans.

In the related area of his career, do those repeated statements that Vince has made about not caring about record sales signify a possible slowing down in his career? To the contrary, he claimed in *Country Weekly* in August of 1998: "I don't want to slow down. The truth of the matter is that this business tells you when you're done. You don't get to dictate when you're done, so I'm just having fun while it's still going."

Although Gill didn't release a new album of his own in 1999, he made several appearances on other albums. Probably the most well-publicized performance he made on record that year was his duet with Barbra Streisand, on her all-ballad album, *A Love Like Ours.* Sharing lead vocals on the Richard Marx composition, "If You Ever Leave Me," Vince sounds wonderful on this lushly orchestrated ballad of love and devotion. Wrote Streisand in the liner notes to that album, "It was great working with Vince Gill, who has such a beautiful voice and is an absolute doll."

The song was written especially for this album, by Marx. Apparently, Streisand asked rock-'n'-roll-oriented Marx if he had ever composed a country song. When he told her he hadn't, he suggested a title like "If You Ever Leave Me, Can I Come Too?" Barbra was highly amused by the idea, and so the song came together. Vince's appearance on this million-selling Streisand disc widened his listening audience even further. Although the number was supposed to be "country," the finished product is more of a beautiful pop ballad than a country entry. Nevertheless, the results are fabulous.

Vince was also one of the singing stars to grace the soundtrack album of Kevin Costner's 1999 baseball flick, *For Love of the Game.* It is a highly varied album of decidedly non-country music, some of it old, some of it new, and some new versions of old tunes. In the later category, Lyle Lovett croons a smooth version of the Frank Sinatra classic, "Summer Wind," Jonny Lang rips his way through the Rolling Stones' "Paint It Black," and Trisha Yearwood sings a sweet version of Paul Simon's "Something So Right" from his 1973 album *There Goes Rhymin' Simon.* Also on the soundtrack album for this romantic/sports film are classic rock cuts from Steely Dan and the late Roy Orbison. Into this fascinating melange of songs, along comes Gill. Vince sings Rodney Crowell's "Loving You Makes Me a Better Man." Sung to a rhythm machine and acoustic guitars, on this song Vince delves further into his pop ballad mode, again proving that he possesses one of the greatest male voices of the era, whether he sings country music or not.

Vince's one country music venture during 1999 was his appearance on Asleep at the Wheel's second tribute to the great country swing master, Bob Wills. The all-star album (*Ride with Bob,* DreamWorks) brought together another stellar cast of the Who's Who of country music, including Willie Nelson, Reba McEntire, Shawn Colvin, Tracy Byrd, the Dixie Chicks, Clint Black, Waylon Jennings, and Lyle Lovett, with modern swing meisters such as the Manhattan Transfer and Squirrel Nut Zippers. Vince plays guitar on the song "Bob's Breakdowns."

In spite of his many accomplishments, Vince Gill remains very much a modest man in an immodest business. As he once told *Country Fever* in mid-1994: "I don't think enough of myself to say, 'I hope people look at me and think, "I'd like to be like him." ' That's sort of an egotistical statement. It's kind of odd, because as long as all those other people are out there like Merle, George, Conway Twitty, and everybody who taught me how to do this, I will always feel like a student. The real meaning in that statement was that I would rather have the respect than any hit record."

So many stars have a vision of how they want to be remembered long after they are gone. Vince scoffs at that notion, proclaiming for the June 1997 issue of *New Country:* "Gosh, I don't know. I like being normal. If somebody says, 'He's really normal,' I like that better than . . . [assuming the voice of a radio announcer]: 'This is the greatest guitar player that ever lived.' Because, that's just silly. I just wanna be part of the world and make a few folks happy while I'm here."

Vince continues non-stop to lend his talents to the recordings of others, because he thrives on the recording process so much. It is estimated that he has sung on or played guitar on at least 400 records by other artists. So generous is he with his time that *Country Weekly* magazine ran a cover story (May 11, 1999) about him entitled: "Vince Gill—The Man Who Never Says 'No.'"

In the spring of 1999, MCA Records hosted a private press party to celebrate Vince Gill's ten years as an artist on the label. On hand was fellow label star Reba McEntire and her husband/manager, Narvel Blackstock. Without a doubt, Reba and Vince were the reigning stars of MCA's country roster throughout the entire decade of the 1990s.

Also that spring, Gill was involved in one of the most unique promotional events in which he had ever participated. A local radio station in Charleston, West Virginia, advertised a "I Want to Graduate with Vince Gill" competition. High school seniors from the area were asked to send in postcards with the message, "I want to graduate with Vince Gill" written on them. The high school that registered the most responses was to have a special meeting with the country music star. The response to the contest was so great that Vince ended up meeting approximately 150 seniors from three separate area high schools, before his concert at the Charleston Civic Center.

Vince told *Country Weekly* at the time; "It's pretty evident that I like kids. I haven't found that kids across the country have a ton of interest in country music. So it's nice to be where they do." He was correct in that statement, as most high school seniors in the class of 1999 in America were more likely to be interested in Marilyn Manson than Vince Gill!

On May 20 and 21, 1999, Vince became the first performer to play in Denver, Colorado's Fillmore Auditorium. He used profits from the concert as a benefit for the recent shooting tragedy at Columbine High School in a suburb of Denver in Colorado. That same month he was awarded two honors from *Country Weekly* magazine. Gill was crowned as 1999's Favorite Instrumentalist and the magazine's Star with the Biggest Heart Award was conferred on him for his ongoing charitable and humanitarian efforts.

Continuing to be a leading draw on top-notch televised country music events, on June 14, 1999, Vince was among the stars to appear on the TNN/*Music City News Country Awards* telecast from the Nashville Arena. Also starring on the show were such headliners as Faith Hill, Diamond Rio, Alan Jackson, Tim McGraw, and Steve Wariner.

Still juggling his love of music with his adoration of golf, on June 19, 1999, Gill was the celebrity guest on the CBS Sports TV show, *Golf 2000*. When asked what his next big goal was, he claimed that it was to win the Masters golf tournament.

During the summer of 1999, Vince presided over his annual golf tournament, The Vinny, at the Golf Club of Tennessee, located west of Nashville. This time around, the celebrity golfers included Kix Brooks, Mark Wills, Chely Wright, Deana Carter, Ralph Emery, T. Graham Brown, Marty Roe (of Diamond Rio), Rudy Gatlin, Ray Benson (of Asleep at the Wheel), comedian Cledus T. Judd, and George Lindsey—who played Goober on the 1960s TV programs *The Andy Griffith Show* and *Mayberry, R.F.D.* Interestingly enough, Vince's longtime love interest, Amy Grant, was also on hand.

In *Country Weekly* magazine, several of the celebrities were interviewed about their support of this charity event. Said Ray Benson at the time, "I'll do anything Vince wants. I will go anywhere and do anything for Vince Gill. Vinnie is the best!"

In that same article, Nashville's own Ralph Emery proclaimed, "I think Vince Gill has done more to give something back to this community than any entertainer I've ever met."

Throughout the summer of 1999, Vince was on the concert trail, racking up seventy shows across the United States. His opening acts included Jo Dee Messina, Deana Carter, and Sherrié Austin. On that particular road tour, Vince performed at the Universal Amphitheater in Los Angeles. Reviewing the show that evening for the *Hollywood Reporter*, Darryl Mordon judged: "Vince Gill is country music's Eric Clapton, scoring his biggest hits as a romantic balladeer yet able to tear it up in concerts as a masterful guitar player."

On September 22, 1999, Vince was among the nominees in the Country Music Association's annual awards ceremony. In addition, he was also the host of the awards event. Program after program, Vince was establishing himself as a very relaxed, proficient, and entertaining TV host of such events. He told *Country Weekly* (August 17, 1999): "I get the jitters when I host the CMA Awards show because I'm not singing. I'm out there hosting and talking and being something different, and that's a little odd. But the more you do it, the easier it gets. Now I just enjoy it, but I do take on a lot of responsibility. It's the biggest night for country music. I feel like a champ that they want me to go out there and introduce folks. I'm not afraid to screw up. I can laugh at myself and be the first one to say, 'You blew that one.'"

That evening, he was nominated in four out of twelve of the major categories. As Album of the Year, Gill's *The Key* was up against *A Place in the Sun* by Tim McGraw, *Always Never the Same* by George Strait, *Two Teardrops* by Steve Wariner, and *Where Your Road Leads* by Trisha Yearwood.

In the field of Male Vocalist of the Year, Vince was pitted against Alan Jackson, Tim McGraw, George Strait, and Steve Wariner. The songwriter's award—Song of the Year—found Vince and Troy Seals nominated alongside "Don't Laugh at Me" by Allen Shamblin and Steve Seskin, "Husbands and Wives" by Roger

Miller, "Please Remember Me" by Rodney Crowell and Will Jennings, and "This Kiss," which was written by Annie Roboff, Robin Lerner, and Beth Nielsen Chapman.

The category of Vocal Event of the Year is always a fascinating fusion of musical talents, and 1999 proved as intriguing as ever, with Vince being nominated in two competitions. Waylon Jennings, Mel Tillis, Bobby Bare, and Jerry Reed were nominated for their *Old Dogs* album. Emmylou Harris, Linda Ronstadt, and Dolly Parton were up for their second joint album, *Trio II*. The all-star grouping of Clint Black, Joe Diffie, Merle Haggard, Emmylou Harris, Alison Krauss, Patty Loveless, Earl Scruggs, Ricky Skaggs, Marty Stuart, Pam Tillis, Randy Travis, Travis Tritt, and Dwight Yoakam were all nominated for the collaborative song they recorded together, "Same Old Train." New singer Sara Evans was tapped for her "No Place That Far," which featured a guest appearance by Vince Gill. And finally, Vince and Patty Loveless were nominated for "My Kind of Woman/My Kind of Man" from *The Key*.

When the trophies were handed out that night in Nashville, the Album of the Year award went to Tim McGraw, as did the prize for the Male Vocalist of the Year. In the songwriter's category, "This Kiss," which was a huge hit for Faith Hill, became Song of the Year. Although the competition was stiff, when it came time to bestow the prize for Vocal Event of the Year, it went to Vince Gill and Patty Loveless for their popular duet, "My Kind of Woman/My Kind of Man." When he accepted the prize on behalf of the absent Loveless and himself, Gill spoke of the merits of keeping traditional country music alive. "Don't lose sight of our roots!" he exclaimed with trophy in hand.

Vince was in fine form as the program's host. He looked very dapper and spoke eloquently as he made Y2K jokes and quipped with the superstar-filled audience and presenters. When Shania Twain won Entertainer of the Year, he teased, "Well Shania, that oughta shut everybody up—you did it, baby!" referring to the criticism that she had received about not being "country" enough to be a country star. In Patty Loveless's absence, Gill closed the show with a rendition of "My Kind of Woman/My Kind of Man" with his dear friend Dolly Parton.

As an awards show host, Vince perfectly embodies all of the right attributes that are necessary for the task. In contrast, although handsome and appealing, Alan Jackson has much too much "aw shucks" self-consciousness to carry a two-hour nationwide broadcast. George Strait is too shy; Marty Stuart is too hyper; Willie Nelson is too unattractive; and Jeff Foxworthy is so busy doing stand-up comedy that he eclipses an event. Gill is the type of guy who is so natural and appealing, that anyone, who turns on a television set, would be happy to have him in their living room for the entire telecast. He is also confident enough within himself that he can crack jokes and make unrehearsed comments, yet still maintain the authority that a "master of ceremonies" must project.

Vince continued to tour throughout 1999. He ended the year, the decade, and the century with four concert dates at Caesar's Palace in Las Vegas, Nevada. When the new millennium dawned, Gill entered it as one of the reigning voices of the music world, whether he sang country, rock, or pop.

———

With all of his successes, Vince is also able to keep his life in perspective, even when tragedy strikes. Gill told *Country Weekly* in August 1999: "It's good for you as a person to get a little dose of something maybe bad happening in the midst of your accomplishments. In the middle of your success—bang!—somebody comes up and goes, 'Here, take that in your heart.' Your brother died, bang; Conway Twitty died, bang; Roger Miller died. In 1997 I had to deal with the death of my father, divorce, and some serious knee problems. I had to get through a stretch of time that wasn't the greatest. The bad things really bring you right back down to earth in a hurry. In adversity you can tell an awful lot more about a person than you can when things are great. Life's real easy when things are going great, but when they take it all away from you and deal you a little bit of a shot, how [are] you going to react?"

Looking back on the 1990s, Gill assessed in *Upbeat* (January 1998): "It's been a good decade. I like the nineties pretty good. I feel lucky that I've achieved what I've achieved and gotten to do what I've gotten to do. Even more so in the years that were lean, the years I didn't have hits. When I look back, the things I'll always remember are the really kind of oddball gigs, the oddball places we've played at, the only people that showed up were in the opening act. There were several gigs like that where the band outnumbered the people in the audience."

Vince Gill has established himself in the 1990s as country music's ultimate singer/songwriter. He has the ability to dance the fine line between country purity and overall mainstream pop appeal. No matter what material he chooses to sing—whether it is an ode to Nashville such as "Kindly Keep It Country" or a broad-based ballad such as his duet with Barbra Streisand, Vince is always comfortably at ease, totally believable, and musically winning.

He has publicly devoted his time and energies to several charitable causes without being syrupy or pandering. He has been supportive of country music traditions without coming across as an unsophisticated hick. He has no need and no desire to dress or behave like a cowboy just to sell a country song.

Vince has fashioned himself into the quintessential country crooner by playing on the strengths of several of the greatest stars of classic country and mainstream pop music, yet never once does he go out of his way to betray any of his own natural attributes or instincts. His music has the country honesty of Johnny Cash, without the bitterness or dark side. His self-penned ballads are every bit as insightful and touching as anything James Taylor has ever written. Like Garth Brooks, he has the innate ability to select just the right songs to interpret, which are perfectly suited to his own voice. He has the vocal agility to bounce back and forth between lushly orchestrated pop and hillbilly twang in much the same way Patsy Cline could. He has the conviction-laden rock believability of Sting, the respected guitar expertise of Bonnie Raitt, and a voice that possesses the sweetness of David Crosby. He has the charm of Marty Robbins and the approachable warmth and friendliness that Mel Tillis projects. Yet, through all of the comparisons, he remains uniquely true to himself in whatever he does.

Vince has never gone on a "star" trip in his head. He is happy creating music that people like to listen to. "I have a simple lifestyle, and I'm not possessed by acquiring everything I can. I don't feel like I have anything to prove. And I don't feel like I ever have," he told *Country Music* back in late winter 1997.

In November of 1999, the mystery of Vince Gill and Amy Grant finally came to a blossoming conclusion. The couple's first public admission of love came when Amy replied to a journalist's question as to whether or not Vince was her "boyfriend?" According to the *Tennessean*, she took a deep breath and confirmed that the answer was indeed "yes."

The November 29, 1999, issue of *People* magazine reported that since the story broke in the *Tennessean*, the couple had been seen all over Nashville—dining at the local Waffle House, attending church together, and playing together at the local golf courses. The *Star* newspaper photographed them in January 2000 hugging and kissing each other at a golf course in Scottsdale, Arizona, the weekend of Superbowl XXXIV. Obviously, they are now free and happy at last to express their love for each other. In March they announced their engagement. It looks like Vince Gill's albums are likely to make a shift from somber to joyful in the future.

To kick off the new century, Vince was on the list of nominees for the Grammy Awards. His song "Don't Come Cryin' to Me" was nominated as the Best Male Country Vocal Performance and the song "Bob's Breakdowns" from Asleep at the Wheel's *Ride with Bob* album was up for the Best Country Instrumental Performance. On February 23, 2000, Vince's guitar playing on "Bob's Breakdowns" earned him his fourteenth Grammy Award.

What great career plans does Vince have in store for himself? He informed *New Country* in June 1997: "I don't see the future, really. I really do live day to day. I don't know if somebody's telling me the truth when they say, 'Well, it was my goal at this point to sell a million records and win this award and do this and do that.' And, I'm kinda going . . . [gives a dumbfounded look], 'Really? For real? I just wanted to get up today.' That's progress to me—wakin' up, startin' a new day."

Instead, Vince insists, as he told *Country Weekly* in June 1998, "The way I live my life is to just wing it." Obviously, it is a formula that works well for him, and he plans to keep on doing it that way. Throughout the 1990s, Vince Gill created some of the most memorable and some of the most emotionally touching country music of the twentieth century, and happily there is much more to come in the new century. As long as Vince Gill is in Nashville, there will always be an unpredictable wealth of great music, whether it is country, rock, folk, or pop. The only thing predictable about Vince Gill and his music is that it has quality, integrity, and a hell of a lot of heart.

DISCOGRAPHY

Albums As a Solo Artist

1. *TURN ME LOOSE* (RCA RECORDS, 1984)

[Vinyl EP format—originally only six cuts]

[CD edition included two bonus cuts; designated by *]

Produced by Emory L. Gordy Jr.

    1. "Turn Me Loose"
    (Vince Gill)

    2. "Oh Carolina"
    (Randy Albright/Jim Elliot/Mark D. Sanders)

    3. "Don't Say That You Love Me"
    (Vince Gill)

    4. "Waitin' for Your Love" *
    (Vince Gill)

    5. "Half a Chance"
    (Vince Gill)

    6. "Victim of Life's Circumstances"
    (Delbert McClinton)

    7. "'Til the Best Comes Along"
    (Vince Gill)

    8. "Livin' the Way I Do" *
    (Vince Gill)

2. *THE THINGS THAT MATTER* (RCA RECORDS, 1985)

Produced by Emory L. Gordy Jr.

    1. "She Don't Know"
       (Vince Gill)

    2. "With You"
       (Vince Gill)

    3. "Savannah (Don't You Ever Think of Me)"
       (Vince Gill)

    4. "Colder Than Winter"
       (Vince Gill)

    5. "True Love"
       (Vince Gill)

    6. "If It Weren't for Him" [duet with Rosanne Cash]
       (Vince Gill/Rosanne Cash)

    7. "Ain't It Always That Way"
       (Dave Loggins)

    8. "Oklahoma Borderline"
       (Vince Gill/Rodney Crowell/Guy Clark)

3. *THE WAY BACK HOME* (RCA RECORDS, 1987)

Produced by Richard Landis

    1. "Everybody's Sweetheart"
       (Vince Gill)

    2. "The Way Back Home"
       (Vince Gill)

    3. "Cinderella"
       (Reed Nielsen)

    4. "Let's Do Something"
       (Vince Gill/Reed Nielsen)

    5. "The Radio"
       (Vince Gill/Reed Nielsen)

    6. "Baby That's Tough"
       (Vince Gill/Guy Clark)

    7. "Losing Your Love"
       (Vince Gill/Rhonda Kye Fleming/Hank DeVito)

8. "It Doesn't Matter Anymore"
   (Paul Anka)
9. "Something's Missing"
   (Vince Gill/Michael Clark)

4. *The Best of Vince Gill* (RCA Records, 1989)

Produced by Emory L. Gordy Jr., Richard Landis, and Barry Beckett

1. "Turn Me Loose"
   (Vince Gill)
2. "Oh Carolina"
   (Randy Albright/Jim Elliot/Mark D. Sanders)
3. "Victim of Life's Circumstances"
   (Delbert McClinton)
4. "Lucy Dee" [previously unreleased]
   (Steve Earle)
5. "Oklahoma Borderline"
   (Vince Gill/Rodney Crowell/Guy Clark)
6. "Cinderella"
   (Reed Nielsen)
7. "Let's Do Something"
   (Vince Gill/Reed Nielsen)
8. "The Radio"
   (Vince Gill/Reed Nielsen)
9. "I've Been Hearing Things About You" [previously unreleased]
   (Vince Gill)
10. "I Never Knew Lonely" [previously unreleased]
    (Vince Gill)

5. *When I Call Your Name* (MCA Records, 1989)

Produced by Tony Brown

1. "Never Alone"
   (Vince Gill/Rosanne Cash)
2. "Sight for Sore Eyes"
   (Vince Gill/Guy Clark)

3. "Oh Girl (You Know Where to Find Me)"
   (Vince Gill)
4. "Oklahoma Swing" [duet with Reba McEntire]
   (Vince Gill/Tim DuBois)
5. "When I Call Your Name"
   (Vince Gill/Tim DuBois)
6. "Ridin' the Rodeo"
   (Vince Gill/Kostas)
7. "Never Knew Lonely"
   (Vince Gill)
8. "We Won't Dance"
   (Greg Trooper)
9. "We Could Have Been"
   (Don Cook/John Jarvis)
10. "Rita Ballou"
    (Guy Clark)

6. *POCKET FULL OF GOLD* (MCA RECORDS, 1991)

Produced by Tony Brown

1. "I Quit"
   (Vince Gill/Max D. Barnes)
2. "Look at Us"
   (Vince Gill/Max D. Barnes)
3. "Take Your Memory with You"
   (Vince Gill)
4. "Pocket Full of Gold"
   (Vince Gill/Brian Allsmiller)
5. "The Strings That Tie You Down"
   (Vince Gill/Max D. Barnes)
6. "Liza Jane"
   (Vince Gill/Reed Nielson)
7. "If I Didn't Have You in My World"
   (Vince Gill/Jim Weatherly)
8. "A Little Left Over"
   (Vince Gill)

9. "What's a Man to Do"
   (T. J. Knight/Curtis Wright)
10. "Sparkle"
    (Jim Lauderdale/John Leventhal)

7. *I Never Knew Lonely* (RCA Records, 1992)

[Greatest hits]

Produced by Emory L. Gordy Jr., Richard Landis, and Barry Beckett

1. "I Never Knew Lonely"
   (Vince Gill)
2. "What If I Say Goodbye" [previously unreleased]
   (Harlan Howard)
3. "The Way Back Home"
   (Vince Gill)
4. "Livin' the Way I Do"
   (Vince Gill)
5. "Everybody's Sweetheart"
   (Vince Gill)
6. "True Love"
   (Vince Gill)
7. "Losing Your Love"
   (Vince Gill/Rhonda Kye Fleming/Hank DeVito)
8. "Midnight Train" [previously unreleased]
   (Vince Gill)
9. "Colder Than Winter"
   (Vince Gill)

8. *I Still Believe in You* (MCA Records, 1992)

Produced by Tony Brown

1. "Don't Let Our Love Start Slippin' Away"
   (Vince Gill/Peter Wasner)
2. "No Future in the Past"
   (Vince Gill/Carl Jackson)
3. "Nothing Like a Woman"
   (Vince Gill/Reed Nielsen)

4. "Tryin' to Get Over You"
   (Vince Gill)
5. "Say Hello"
   (Vince Gill/Pete Wasner)
6. "One More Last Chance"
   (Vince Gill/Gary Nicholson)
7. "Under These Conditions"
   (Vince Gill/Max D. Barnes)
8. "Pretty Words"
   (Vince Gill/Don Schlitz)
9. "Love Never Broke Anyone's Heart"
   (Vince Gill/Jim Weatherly)
10. "I Still Believe in You"
    (Vince Gill/John Barlow Jarvis)

9. *LET THERE BE PEACE ON EARTH* (MCA RECORDS, 1993)

Produced by Tony Brown

1. "Do You Hear What I Hear"
   (Noel Regney/Gloria Shayne)
2. "Have Yourself a Merry Little Christmas"
   (Hugh Martin/Ralph Blane)
3. "One Bright Star"
   (John Barlow Jarvis)
4. "What Child Is This"
   (traditional)
5. "Santa Claus Is Coming to Town"
   (T. Fred Coots/Haven Gillespie)
6. "I'll Be Home for Christmas"
   (Kim Gannon/Walter Kent/Buck Ram)
7. "Let There Be Peace on Earth"
   [duet with Jenny Gill]
   (traditional)
   (Sy Miller/Jill Jackson)
8. "White Christmas"
   (Irving Berlin)

9. "'Til the Season Comes Around Again"
(John Barlow Jarvis/Randy Goodrum)

10. "It's Won't Be the Same This Year"
(Vince Gill)

10. *WHEN LOVE FINDS YOU* (MCA RECORDS, 1994)

Produced by Tony Brown

1. "Whenever You Come Around"
(Vince Gill/Pete Wasner)

2. "You Better Think Twice"
(Vince Gill/Reed Nielsen)

3. "Real Lady's Man"
(Vince Gill/Carl Jackson)

4. "What the Cowgirls Do"
(Vince Gill/Reed Nielsen)

5. "When Love Finds You"
(Vince Gill/Michael Omartian)

6. "If There's Anything I Can Do"
(Vince Gill/John Barlow Jarvis)

7. "South Side of Dixie"
(Vince Gill/Dilbert McClinton)

8. "Maybe Tonight"
(Vince Gill/Janis Gill)

9. "Which Bridge to Cross (Which Bridge to Burn)"
(Vince Gill/Bill Anderson)

10. "If I Had My Way"
(Vince Gill/Amy Grant)

11. "Go Rest High on That Mountain"
(Vince Gill)

11. *THE ESSENTIAL VINCE GILL* (RCA RECORDS, 1995)

[Greatest hits]

* Produced by Emory L. Gordy Jr.

** Produced by Barry Beckett

*** Produced by Richard Landis

1. "Victim of Life's Circumstances" *
   (Delbert McClinton)
2. "Oh Carolina" *
   (Randy Albright/Jim Elliot/Mark D. Sanders)
3. "I've Been Hearing Things About You" **
   (Vince Gill)
4. "Turn Me Loose" *
   (Vince Gill)
5. "The Radio" ***
   (Vince Gill/Reed Nielsen)
6. "Livin' the Way I Do" *
   (Vince Gill)
7. "Midnight Train" **
   (Vince Gill)
8. "True Love" *
   (Vince Gill)
9. "Ain't It Always That Way" *
   (Dave Loggins)
10. "Oklahoma Borderline" *
    (Vince Gill/Rodney Crowell/Guy Clark)
11. "With You" *
    (Vince Gill)
12. "The Way Back Home" ***
    (Vince Gill)
13. "Losing Your Love" ***
    (Vince Gill/Rhonda Kye Fleming/Hank DeVito)
14. "Everybody's Sweetheart" ***
    (Vince Gill)
15. "Don't Say That You Love Me" *
    (Vince Gill/Emory L. Gordy Jr.)
16. "Something's Missing" ***
    (Vince Gill/Michael Clark)
17. "Colder Than Winter" *
    (Vince Gill)

18. "Cinderella" ***
    (Reed Nielsen)
19. "Let's Do Something" ***
    (Vince Gill/Reed Nielsen)
20. "I Never Knew Lonely" **
    (Vince Gill)

12. SOUVENIRS (MCA RECORDS, 1995)

[Greatest hits]

Produced by Tony Brown

    * Produced by Tony Brown and Reba McEntire

** Produced by Steve Buckingham and Dolly Parton

1. "Never Alone"
   (Vince Gill/Rosanne Cash)
2. "Never Knew Lonely"
   (Vince Gill)
3. "When I Call Your Name"
   (Vince Gill/Tim DuBois)
4. "Liza Jane"
   (Vince Gill/Reed Nielsen)
5. "Look at Us"
   (Vince Gill/Max D. Barnes)
6. "Take Your Memory with You"
   (Vince Gill)
7. "Pocket Full of Gold"
   (Vince Gill/Brian Allsmiller)
8. "The Heart Won't Lie"
   [duet with Reba McEntire] *
   (Kim Carnes/Donna Terry Weiss)
9. "Don't Let Our Love Start Slippin' Away"
   (Vince Gill/Pete Wasner)
10. "I Still Believe in You"
    (Vince Gill/John Barlow Jarvis)

11. "No Future in the Past"
    (Vince Gill/Carl Jackson)
12. "Tryin' to Get Over You"
    (Vince Gill)
13. "One More Last Chance"
    (Vince Gill/Gary Nicholson)
14. "I Can't Tell You Why"
    (Don Henley/Glen Frey/Timothy B. Schmit)
15. "I Will Always Love You" with Dolly Parton **
    (Dolly Parton)

13. *VINCE GILL SUPER HITS* (RCA RECORDS, 1996)

[Greatest hits]

Produced by Emory L. Gordy Jr., Barry Beckett, and Richard Landis

1. "I Never Knew Lonely"
   (Vince Gill)
2. "Oklahoma Borderline"
   (Vince Gill/Rodney Crowell/Guy Clark)
3. "Losing Your Love"
   (Vince Gill/Rhonda Kye Fleming/Hank DeVito)
4. "Half a Chance"
   (Vince Gill)
5. "Cinderella"
   (Reed Nielsen)
6. "The Radio"
   (Vince Gill/Reed Nielsen)
7. "Savannah (Don't You Ever Think of Me)"
   (Vince Gill)
8. "With You"
   (Vince Gill)
9. "Baby That's Tough"
   (Vince Gill/Guy Clark)
10. "Everybody's Sweetheart"
    (Vince Gill)

14. *HIGH LONESOME SOUND* (MCA RECORDS, 1996)

Produced by Tony Brown

1. "One Dance with You"
   (Vince Gill/Reed Nielsen)
2. "High Lonesome Sound"
   (Vince Gill)
3. "Pretty Little Adriana"
   (Vince Gill)
4. "A Little More Love"
   (Vince Gill)
5. "Down to New Orleans"
   (Vince Gill/Peter Wasner)
6. "Tell Me Lover"
   (Vince Gill)
7. "Given More Time"
   (Vince Gill/Don Schlitz)
8. "You and You Alone"
   (Vince Gill)
9. "World's Apart"
   (Vince Gill/Bob DiPiero)
10. "Jenny Dreamed of Trains"
    (Vince Gill/Guy Clark)
11. "High Lonesome Sound"
    [version two, featuring Alison Krauss & Union Station]
    (Vince Gill)

15. *VINTAGE GILL—THE ENCORE COLLECTION* (BMG RECORDS, 1997)

[Repackage of RCA songs]

[CD edition included bonus cuts; designated by *]

Produced by Emory L. Gordy Jr., Barry Beckett, and Richard Landis

1. "I Never Knew Lonely"
   (Vince Gill)
2. "Oh Carolina"
   (Randy Albright/Jim Elliot/Mark D. Sanders)

3. "Let's Do Something"
(Vince Gill/Reed Nielsen)
4. "The Radio"
(Vince Gill/Reed Nielsen)
5. "Oklahoma Borderline"
(Vince Gill/Rodney Crowell/Guy Clark)
6. "It Doesn't Matter Anymore"
(Paul Anka)
7. "Baby That's Tough"
(Vince Gill/Guy Clark)
8. "'Til the Best Comes Along"
(Vince Gill)
9. "What If I Say Goodbye" *
(Vince Gill)
10. "The Way Back Home" *
(Vince Gill)

16. *VINCE GILL AND FRIENDS* **(BMG RECORDS, 1998)**

[Repackage of RCA songs]

Produced by Emory L. Gordy Jr., Barry Beckett, and Richard Landis

1. "Turn Me Loose"
[background vocals by Janis Oliver Gill and Herb Pedersen]
(Vince Gill)
2. "What If I Say Goodbye"
[background vocals by Emmylou Harris]
(Harlan Howard)
3. "Oklahoma Borderline"
[background vocals by Rodney Crowell and Herb Pedersen]
(Vince Gill/Rodney Crowell/Guy Clark)
4. "The Way Back Home"
[background vocals by Emmylou Harris and Bonnie Raitt]
(Vince Gill)
5. "Let's Do Something" [background vocals by Bonnie Raitt]
(Vince Gill/Reed Nielsen)

6. "Oh Carolina"
   [background vocals by Emmylou Harris and Carl Jackson]
   (Randy Albright/Jim Elliot/Mark Sanders)
7. "Don't Say That You Love Me"
   [background vocals by Janis Oliver Gill]
   (Vince Gill/Emory L. Gordy Jr.)
8. "Everybody's Sweetheart"
   [background vocals by Sweethearts of the Rodeo]
   (Vince Gill)

17. *The Key* (MCA Records, 1998)

Produced by Tony Brown

1. "Don't Come Cryin' to Me"
   (Vince Gill/Reed Nielsen)
2. "If You Ever Have Forever in Mind"
   (Vince Gill/Troy Seals)
3. "I Never Really Knew You"
   (Vince Gill)
4. "Kindly Keep It Country"
   (Vince Gill)
5. "All Those Years"
   (Vince Gill)
6. "I'll Take Texas"
   (Vince Gill)
7. "My Kind of Woman/My Kind of Man" [duet with Patty Loveless]
   (Vince Gill)
8. "There's Not Much Love Here Anymore"
   (Vince Gill)
9. "Let Her In"
   (Vince Gill)
10. "The Hills of Caroline"
    (Vince Gill)
11. "Live to Tell It All"
    (Vince Gill/Sonya Isaacs)

12. "What They All Call Love"
    (Vince Gill)
13. "The Key to Life"
    (Vince Gill)

18. *BREATH OF HEAVEN* (MCA RECORDS, 1998)

Produced by Tony Brown and Michael Omartian

1. "Winter Wonderland"
   (Felix Bernard/Richard Smith)
2. "The Christmas Song"
   (Mel Torme/Richard Wells)
3. "O Little Town of Bethlehem"
   (traditional)
4. "Silver Bells"
   (Jay Livingston/Ray Evans)
5. "It's the Most Wonderful Time of the Year"
   (George Wyle/Eddie Pola)
6. "Blue Christmas"
   (Billy Hayes/Jay W. Johnson)
7. "O Holy Night"
   (traditional)
8. "Let It Snow, Let It Snow, Let It Snow"
   (Sammy Cahn/Jule Styne)
9. "A Cradle in Bethlehem"
   (Al Bryan/Lawrence Stock)
10. "Breath of Heaven (Mary's Song)"
    (Amy Grant/Chris Eaton)
11. "O Come All Ye Faithful"
    (traditional)

As a Member of the Group Pure Praire League

1. *Can't Hold Back* (RCA Records, 1979)

Produced by Ron Albert and Howard Albert

    1. "I Can't Hold Back"
       (Vince Gill)
    2. "I Can't Believe"
       (Vince Gill)
    3. "Rude Rude Awakening"
       (Miller)
    4. "White Line"
       (Bennett)
    5. "Misery Train"
       (Vince Gill)
    6. "Restless Woman"
       (Patrick Bolen/Michael Reilly)
    7. "I'm Goin' Away"
       (Vince Gill)
    8. "Jerene"
       (Vince Gill)
    9. "Livin' It Alone"
       (Patrick Bolen)
   10. "Fool Fool"
       (Seals/McBee/Barnes)
   11. "Goodbye So Long"
       (Patrick Bolen/Michael Reilly)

2. *Firin' Up* (Casablanca Records, 1980)

Produced by John Ryan

    1. "I'm Almost Ready"
       (Vince Gill)
    2. "Give It Up"
       (D. Lubahan/W. Fritzsching)

3. "Too Many Heartaches in Paradise"
(J. Wilson/D. Greer)

4. "She's All Mine"
(Vince Gill)

5. "You're My True Love"
(Vince Gill)

6. "Let Me Love You Tonight"
(Jeff Wilson/Dan Greer/Steve Woodard)

7. "I Can't Stop This Feelin'"
(D. Flower/J. Sanderfur)

8. "Lifetime of Nighttime"
(Vince Gill)

9. "I'll Be Damned"
(Vince Gill)

10. "Janny Lou"
(Vince Gill)

3. SOMETHING IN THE NIGHT (CASABLANCA RECORDS, 1981)
Produced by Rob Fraboni

1. "Don't Keep Me Hangin'"
(Vince Gill)

2. "Love Me Again"
(Vince Gill)

3. "Hold On to Our Hearts"
(Vince Gill)

4. "Something in the Night"
(Dan Greer/Jeff Wilson/Steve Woodard)

5. "Do You Love Me Truly, Julie?"
(Vince Gill)

6. "You're Mine Tonight"
(Rafe Van Hoy)

7. "Still Right Here in My Heart"
(Jeff Wilson/Dan Greer)

8. "I Wanna Know Your Name"
(Vince Gill)

9. "Feel the Fire"
   (Dan Greer/Jeff Wilson/Steve Woodard)
10. "Tell Me One More Time"
    (Dan Greer/Jeff Wilson)

4. *THE BEST OF PURE PRAIRIE LEAGUE* BY *PURE PRAIRIE LEAGUE* (POLYGRAM RECORDS, 1995)

* Produced by Rob Fraboni

** Produced by John Ryan

Non-Vince Gill cuts:

1. "Amie"
2. "Falling In and Out of Love"
3. "That'll Be the Day"
4. "Two Lane Highway"

Vince Gill cuts:

5. "Let Me Love You Tonight" **
   (Jeff Wilson/Dan Greer/Steve Woodard)
6. "I'm Almost Ready" **
   (Vince Gill)
7. "I Can't Stop This Feelin'" **
   (D. Flower/J. Sanderfur)
8. "Still Right Here in My Heart" *
   (Jeff Wilson/Dan Greer)
9. "You're Mine Tonight" *
   (Rafe Van Hoy)
10. "I'll Be Damned" **
    (Vince Gill)
11. "Something in the Night" *
    (Dan Greer/Jeff Wilson/Steve Woodard)
12. "Janny Lou" **
    (Vince Gill)
13. "Tell Me One More Time" *
    (Dan Greer/Jeff Wilson)

Vince Gill Appearances on Other Albums

[Only the specific Vince Gill songs are listed. The producer listed refers to the producer of Vince Gill's song(s) on the respective album, which may be different than the producer(s) of the rest of the album.]

GREEN LIGHT BY BONNIE RAITT (WARNER BROS. RECORDS, 1982)
Produced by Rob Fabroni
"I Can't Help Myself"
[background vocals by Johnny Lee Schell, Bonnie Raitt, Vince Gill]
(Johnny Lee Schell/Bonnie Raitt/Ricky Fataar/Ray O'Hara)

SWEETHEARTS OF THE RODEO BY SWEETHEARTS OF THE RODEO (COLUMBIA RECORDS, 1986)
Produced by Steve Buckingham
Vince plays guitar throughout the album.

ONE TIME/ONE NIGHT BY SWEETHEARTS OF THE RODEO (COLUMBIA RECORDS, 1988)
Produced by Steve Buckingham
Vince plays guitar throughout the album.

NEW NASHVILLE CATS BY MARK O'CONNOR (WARNER BROS. RECORDS, 1991)
Produced by Ed Norman
"Restless" [with Mark O'Connor, Steve Wariner, and Ricky Skaggs]

ON EVERY STREET BY DIRE STRAITS (WARNER BROS. RECORDS, 1991)
Produced by Mark Knopfler
Vince plays guitar throughout the album.

IT'S YOUR CALL BY REBA MCENTIRE (MCA RECORDS, 1992)

Produced by Tony Brown and Reba McEntire
> "The Heart Won't Lie"
> [duet by Reba McEntire and Vince Gill]
> (Kim Carnes/Donna Terry Weiss)

WALLS CAN FALL BY GEORGE JONES (MCA RECORDS, 1992)

Produced by Emory L. Gordy Jr.
> "I Don't Need No Rockin' Chair"
> [featuring George Jones with Vince Gill, Mark Chesnutt, Garth
> Brooks, Travis Tritt, Joe Diffie, Alan Jackson, Pam Tillis, T. Graham
> Brown, Patty Loveless, and Clint Black]
> (Dycus/Phillips/Yates)

HONEYMOON IN VEGAS (EPIC RECORDS, 1992)

[Soundtrack]
Produced by Tony Brown
> "That's All Right"
> (Arthur Crudup)

SISTERS BY SWEETHEARTS OF THE RODEO (COLUMBIA RECORDS, 1992)

Produced by Steve Buckingham and Wendy Waldman
> Vince plays guitar throughout the album and is also heard as a back-
> ground singer.

**COMMON THREAD: THE SONGS OF THE EAGLES BY VARIOUS ARTISTS
(GIANT RECORDS, 1993)**

Produced by Tony Brown
> "I Can't Tell You Why"
> (Frey/Henley)

INDECENT PROPOSAL BY VARIOUS ARTISTS (MCA RECORDS, 1993)

[Soundtrack]
Produced by Tony Brown

"What Do You Want the Girl to Do"
[duet by Little Feat and Vince Gill]
(Allen Toussaint)

ANOTHER ANGEL GETS ITS WINGS (MCA RECORDS, 1993)
Duet with Trisha Yearwood
[Special bonus cassette, available through Target department stores]
(written/produced by Robert Irving and Kevin Quinn)

A TRIBUTE TO THE MUSIC OF BOB WILLS BY ASLEEP AT THE WHEEL (LIBERTY RECORDS, 1993)
Produced by Ray Benson
"Red Wing" [featuring Vince Gill on electric guitar]
(Mills/Chattaway)
"Yearning (Just for You)" [lead vocal by Vince Gill]
(Benny Carter/Joseph Burke)

RODEO WALTZ BY SWEETHEARTS OF THE RODEO (SUGAR HILL RECORDS, 1993)
Produced by Janis Gill
Vince appears throughout the album as a guitar player and also is heard as a background singer.

8 SECONDS (MCA RECORDS, 1994)
[Soundtrack]
Produced by Andrew Gold and Kenny Edwards
"When Will I Be Loved" [duet by Vince Gill and Karla Bonoff]
(Phil Everly)

MAMA'S HUNGRY EYES: A TRIBUTE TO MERLE HAGGARD BY VARIOUS ARTISTS (ARISTA RECORDS, 1994)
Produced by Tony Brown
"A Farmer's Daughter"
(Merle Haggard)

RHYTHM, COUNTRY AND BLUES BY VARIOUS ARTISTS (MCA
RECORDS, 1994)
Produced by Don Was
    "Ain't Nothing Like the Real Thing"
    [duet by Gladys Knight and Vince Gill]
    (Nickolas Ashford/Valerie Simpson)

MAVERICK BY VARIOUS ARTISTS (ATLANTIC RECORDS, 1994)
[Soundtrack]
Produced by Michael Omartian
    "Ophelia"
    (Robbie Robertson)

HOUSE OF LOVE BY AMY GRANT (A&M RECORDS, 1994)
Produced by Keith Thomas
    "House of Love" [duet by Amy Grant and Vince Gill]
    (Wally Wilson/Kenny Greenberg/Greg Barnhill)

SOMETHING SPECIAL BY DOLLY PARTON (COLUMBIA RECORDS, 1995)
Produced by Steve Buckingham
    "I Will Always Love You" [duet by Dolly Parton and Vince Gill]
    (Dolly Parton)

A FIDDLE AND A SONG BY BYRON BERLINE (SUGAR HILL RECORDS, 1995)
    "Rose of Old Kentucky" [duet by Byron Berline and Vince Gill]
    (Byron Berline)

ONE VOICE BY VARIOUS ARTISTS (MCA RECORDS, 1996)
Produced by Michael Omartian
    "Atlanta Reel '96"
    [featuring Michael Omartian, Vince Gill, Chet Atkins, Alison
    Krauss, Bela Fleck, and Paul Franklin]
    (Michael Omartian)

BEKKA & BILLY BY BEKKA BRAMLETT AND BILLY BURNETTE (UNI RECORDS, 1997)
Produced by Garth Fundis
    Vince plays the electric guitar on the album.

TRIBUTE TO TRADITION BY VARIOUS ARTISTS (COLUMBIA RECORDS, 1998)
Produced by Vince Gill
    "Wine, Women, and Song" [duet by Patti Loveless and Vince Gill]
    (Patti Loveless)

CROWN OF JEWELS BY RANDY SCRUGGS (REPRISE RECORDS, 1998)
Produced by Randy Scruggs
    "A Soldier's Joy" [duet by Randy Scruggs and Vince Gill]
    (Randy Scruggs/Vince Gill)

PRINCE OF EGYPT—NASHVILLE BY VARIOUS ARTISTS (DREAMWORKS RECORDS, 1998)
Produced by Vince Gill and Tony Brown
    "Once in Awhile"
    (Vince Gill/Reed Nielsen)

FAITH BY FAITH HILL (WARNER BROS. RECORDS, 1998)
Produced by Faith Hill, Dan Huff, and Byron Gillimore
    Vince is heard throughout the album on background vocals.

FOR LOVE OF THE GAME (MCA RECORDS, 1999)
[Soundtrack]
Produced by Tony Brown and Rodney Crowell
    "Loving You Makes Me a Better Man"
    (Rodney Crowell)

***RIDE WITH BOB* BY ASLEEP AT THE WHEEL (UNI/DREAMWORKS RECORDS, 1999)**
Produced by Ray Benson
    "Bob's Breakdowns" [Vince Gill featured on guitar]
    (arranged by Ray Benson and Jason Roberts)

***A LOVE LIKE OURS* BY BARBRA STREISAND (COLUMBIA RECORDS, 1999)**
Cut produced by David Foster and Richard Marx
    "If You Ever Leave Me" [duet by Barbra Streisand and Vince Gill]
    (Richard Marx)

VIDEOGRAPHY

V i d e o s

"Turn Me Loose" (RCA Records, 1984)

"Never Knew Lonely" (MCA Records, 1990)

"Pocket Full of Gold" (MCA Records, 1990)

"When I Call Your Name" (MCA Records, 1990)

"Liza Jane" (MCA Records, 1991)

"Look at Us" (MCA Records, 1991)

"Don't Let Our Love Start Slippin' Away" (MCA Records, 1992)

"I Still Believe in You" (MCA Records, 1992)

"Have Yourself a Merry Little Christmas" (MCA Records, 1993)

"The Heart Won't Lie" (MCA Records, 1993) [Vince Gill and Reba McEntire]

"One More Last Chance" (MCA Records, 1993)

"Tryin' to Get Over You" (MCA Records, 1994)

"What the Cowgirls Do" (MCA Records, 1994)

"When Love Finds You" (MCA Records, 1994)

"Go Rest High on That Mountain" (MCA Records, 1995)

"World's Apart" (MCA Records, 1996)

"A Little More Love" (MCA Records, 1997)

"You and You Alone" (MCA Records, 1997)

"If You Ever Have Forever in Mind" (MCA Records, 1998)

"My Kind of Woman/My Kind of Man" (MCA Records, 1999) [Vince Gill and Patty Loveless]

Video Packages

I Still Believe in You (MCA, 1992) VHS and Laserdisc
Christmas with Vince Gill (MCA, 1994) VHS and Laserdisc
Souvenirs—Live at the Ryman (MCA, 1996) VHS

FILMOGRAPHY

8 Seconds (NEW LINE CINEMA, 1994). 104 MINUTES, PG-13.
DIRECTOR: John G. Avildsen.
CAST: Luke Perry (Lane Frost); Stephen Baldwin (Tuff Hedeman); Cynthia Geary (Kellie Frost); Red Mitchell (Cody Lambert); James Rebhorn (Clyde Frost); Carrie Snodgress (Elsie Frost); Ronnie Claire Edwards (Carolyn Kyle); Cameron Finley (Young Lane); Dustin Mayfield (Teenage Lane); Linden Ashby (Martin Hudson); Renee Zellweger (Prescott Motel Buckle Bunny); Vince Gill (Wedding Singer at Reception); Karla Bonoff Band (Themselves).

Maverick (WARNER BROS., 1994). 129 MINUTES, PG.
DIRECTOR: Richard Donner.
CAST: Mel Gibson (Bret Maverick); Jodie Foster (Annabelle Bransford); James Garner (Zane Cooper); Graham Greene (Joseph); Alfred Molina (Angel); James Coburn (Commodore); Dub Taylor (Room Clerk); Geoffrey Lewis (Matthew Wicker); Paul L. Smith (Archduke); Dan Hedaya (Twitchy); Dennis Fimple (Stuttering); Denver Pyle (Old Gambler); Clint Black (Sweet-faced Gambler); Max Perlich (Johnny Hardin); Hal Ketuchm, Corey Feldman, John Woodward (Bank Robbers), Waylon Jennings and Kathy Mattea (Couple with Concealed Guns); Carlene Carter (Waitress); Vince Gill and Janis Gill (Spectators on the Riverboat); Danny Glover (Bank Robber).

FACTS

Full name: Vincent Grant Gill

Birth date: April 12, 1957

Birthplace: Norman, Oklahoma

Hair: Black

Eyes: Hazel, with long lashes

Height/weight: 6 foot 3 inches, 190 pounds

Voice: Tenor

Hat: No cowboy hats, only baseball or golf caps

Clothes: Prefers to dress for comfort—Hawaiian shirts, shorts, flip-flops, jeans

Children: Jenny, born May 5, 1982

Parents: Father—Stan, died July 27, 1997

      Mother—Jerene, homemaker, hairdresser

Family: Older Brother—Bob, died of heart failure, 1993

      Younger Sister—Gina

Earliest talent facts: Age six played guitar; first guitar at ten; by fifteen in bluegrass band, Mountain Smoke

Influences: Bill Monroe, Chet Atkins, The Beatles, Led Zeppelin, Canned Heat, Jim Reeves, Patsy Cline, Buck Owens, Merle Haggard

Instruments: Guitar, banjo, piano, mandolin, fiddle, Dobro

TOUR SITES AND ADDRESSES

If you are interested in traveling to any of the Vince Gill sites or viewing Gill-oriented displays, the following information will be invaluable to you.

CALIFORNIA
Country Star Restaurant
Owned by Vince Gill, Reba McEntire, Wynonna Judd, Lorraine Crook, Charlie Chase, and Alan Jackson. This theme restaurant features memorabilia from all of the stars and great country barbecue style food. It is part of the Walk of Fame at Universal Studios, in Universal City. In the Los Angeles area, take the 101 or the 134 freeway to Lankershim Boulevard. Phone: (818) 762-3939.

OKLAHOMA
Bob Wood's Del City Music Store
Several celebrities have left their footprints and autographs here including Gill. Located in the same area as Oklahoma Country-Western Hall of Fame and Museum. Address: 2908 Epperly, Del City, Oklahoma. Phone: (405) 677-8777.

OKLAHOMA COUNTRY-WESTERN HALL OF FAME AND MUSEUM
Honoring several legends of country music in displays and tributes, including Vince Gill, Reba McEntire, Bob Wills, and Garth Brooks. Address: 3925 29th Street, Del City, Oklahoma. Phone: (405) 677-3174.

TENNESSEE

The Bluebird Café

Vince Gill once performed here at the beginning of his Nashville recording career. Other notables who have played here on their way to success are Garth Brooks, Kathy Mattea, and Leroy Parnell. The Bluebird was also immortalized in the film *The Thing Called Love* (1993). Address: 4104 Hillsboro Road, Nashville, Tennessee. Phone: (615) 383-1461.

GILL & ARNOLD BOUTIQUE

This is the store that Vince helped pay for and which is presided over by his ex-wife, Janis, and her sister. This Sweethearts of the Rodeo shop is perfect for cowgirls who get the blues! It is located at 334 Main Street, Franklin, Tennessee. Phone: (615) 791-1207.

THE GRAND OLE OPRY MUSEUM

What was once a national radio program broadcasting on WSM from the historic Ryman Auditorium in downtown Nashville is now a multimillion-dollar complex outside the city. On display is an array of country music history of the past and present. In the museum are several displays including country legend Patsy Cline's famed den furniture, as well as memorabilia from contemporary stars such as Vince Gill. Address: 2800 Opryland Drive, Nashville, Tennessee. Phone: (615) 889-1000.

SITES ON THE INTERNET

COUNTRY.COM—VINCE GILL

Biography, career statistics, photos.

www.country.com/gen/music/artist/vince_gill.html

COUNTRY MUSIC NEWS—COUNTRYCOOL.COM—VINCE GILL

News about Vince's charity golf events.

www.countrycool.com/news/09/30a.html

ERIC'S VINCE GILL PAGE

Tribute to Vince Gill with photographs from Nashville.

edge.net~whitem/vince.htm

GREAT AMERICAN COUNTRY—VINCE GILL

Biography, press releases, photos, maintained by GAC TV network.

www.countrystars.com/artists/vgill.html

IMUSIC COUNTRY SHOWCASE—VINCE GILL

Vince Gill photos, audio clips, bio, album info, and bulletin board.

imusic.com/showcase2/country/merch/vin

KAREN'S VINCE GILL PHOTO ALBUM

Vince Gill concert photos from Syracuse, New York, September 1998.
www.hi-tek.net/photo8.html

LIGHTHOUSE ARTIST DATABASE VINCE GILL

Biographical and career information.
tlem.netcentral.net/cmr/database/g/gil

SKREW—VINCE GILL MERCHANDISE

Vince Gill Official Merchandise for sale, including T-shirts
and other items.
www.skrew.com/merch_bands_vincegill.ht

TigerX VINCE GILL SITE

Biographical and career news on Vince Gill.
www.tigerx.com/people/gill.htm

TOTALLY ConVINCE'd

Biography, discography, photos, concert reviews, Vince Gill chat
room.
www.geocities.com/Nashville/6900/vincegill.html
or
www.hitek.net/vincegill.html

THE VINCE GILL BASKETBALL GAME AND CONCERT 1997

Photos and information on the Vince Gill Celebrity Basketball Game
and Concert benefiting the Mike Curb Music Business Program
and the Athletic Department of Belmont University, Nashville,
Tennessee. Monday, November 3, 1997, updated October 16, 1998.
times-herald.com/ag/amy13

VINCE GILL OFFICIAL WEB SITE

Biography and press releases about Vince Gill and his career.
www.vincegill.com

VINCE GILL ON CD NOW

Biography on Vince Gill, links to purchase albums on CD, cassette, and videos. Also links to magazine articles on Vince.

www.cdnow.com (then key in Vince Gill in Artist Search box)

VINCE GILL ON LYCOS ROLLING STONE.COM

Biography on Vince Gill, plus links to illustrated biography, compiled by *Rolling Stone* magazine.

rollingstone.lycos.com/artists/bio/asp?ArtistID=3118

VINCE GILL ON SONIC NET

Biography, discography, audio clips, album reviews.

www.sonicnet.com/artistinfo/150207.jhtml?_requestid=139233

VINCEWORLD!

News, reviews, photos, and Vince Gill Internet links.

www.vinceworld.net/

VINNY FANS CHAT ROOM . . . FROM THE UNOFFICIAL VINCE GILL FAN SITE

Mailing list, photos, bio, chat, discography, message board.

www.specialweb.com/vinnyfans/chat.html

VINNY FANS—THE UNOFFICIAL VINCE GILL FAN SITE

Contests, discography, message board maintained by Celine Chamberlin.

www.specialweb.com/vinnyfans

AWARDS

[Note: The years referred to in this list in some instances indicate the year in which the award was presented, as is the case of the Country Music Association Awards. With other awards, however, including the Grammys, the year refers to the previous year, in which the recording was on the charts. There is no unifying standard.]

Academy of Country Music Awards

1984	New Male Vocalist of the Year
1992	Top Male Vocalist of the Year
1992	Song of the Year, "I Still Believe in You"
1993	Top Male Vocalist of the Year

American Music Awards

1994	Country Single of the Year, "Whenever You Come Around"

Billborad Magazine Top Ten Hits, Year-by-Year

1980	"Let Me Love You Tonight"
	[Vince Gill with Pure Prairie League]

1985   "If It Weren't for Him" [Vince Gill and Rosanne Cash]
          "Oklahoma Borderline"

1987   "Cinderella"

1990   "Never Knew Lonely"
          "When I Call Your Name"

1991   "Pocket Full of Gold"
          "Liza Jane"
          "Look at Us"

1992   "Don't Let Our Love Start Slippin' Away"
          "I Still Believe in You"
          "Take Your Memory with You"

1993   "The Heart Won't Lie" [Vince Gill and Reba McEntire]
          "No Future in the Past"
          "What the Cowgirls Do"
          "When Love Finds You"

1994   "Tryin' to Get Over You"
          "What the Cowgirls Do"
          "When Love Finds You"
          "Whenever You Come Around"

1995   "Which Bridge to Cross (Which Bridge to Burn)"
          "You Better Think Twice"

1996   "Pretty Little Adriana"
          "Worlds Apart"

1997   "A Little More Love"
          "You and You Alone"

1998   "If You Ever Have Forever in Mind"

BMI Songwriter's Awards

1987   Most Performed Songs, "If It Weren't for Him," "Oklahoma Borderline"

1991   Most Performed Songs, "I Never Knew Lonely," "Oklahoma Swing," "When I Call Your Name"

1992   Most Performed Songs, "Here We Are," "I Still Believe in You," "Liza Jane," "Look at Us," "Pocket Full of Gold"

1992   Songwriter of the Year

1993   Most Performed Songs, "Don't Let Our Love Start Slippin' Away,"
        "I Still Believe in You," "Take Your Memory with You"

1995   Songwriter of the Year

1996   Humanitarian Award

1996   Most Performed Songs, "Which Bridge to Cross (Which Bridge
        to Burn)," "You Better Think Twice"

1997   Most Performed Songs, "Go Rest High on That Mountain,"
        "Pretty Little Adriana"

Charity and Benefit Awards

[Vince Gill has been honored by the following organizations]

American Heart Association

Baptist Hospital (Nashville, Tennessee)

Belmont College (Nashville, Tennessee)

Cerebral Palsy Foundation

The Ear Foundation

Easter Seals

Feed The Children

The Jimmy Everest Cancer Center

Kidney Foundation

Make-a-Wish Foundation

Mama's Hungry Eyes

Mercy Homes

The National Coalition for the Homeless

Pregnancy Crisis Center (Nashville, Tennessee)

The Relief Fund of the Red Cross

Sara Lee Classic

Special Care, Children's Disabilities

T. J. Martell Foundation

UMC Children's Pediatric Intensive Care Unit

The Vinny Pro-Celebrity Golf Invitational

Walden Pond Project, Rain Forest Fund

Country Music Association Awards

[Note: Vince Gill has won more CMA Awards than any other recipient in the history of the association to date]

1990 Song of the Year, "When I Call Your Name"
1991 Male Vocalist of the Year
1991 Song of the Year, "When I Call Your Name"
1991 Vocal Event of the Year, "Restless"
   [Vince Gill, Mark O'Connor, Steve Wariner, and Ricky Skaggs]
1992 Male Vocalist of the Year
1992 Song of the Year, "Look at Us"
1993 Album of the Year, *I Still Believe in You*
1993 Entertainer of the Year
1993 Male Vocalist of the Year
1993 Song of the Year, "I Still Believe in You"
1993 Vocal Event of the Year, "I Don't Need Your Rockin' Chair"
   [George Jones with Vince Gill, Mark Chesnutt, Garth Brooks,
   Travis Tritt, Joe Diffie, Alan Jackson, Pam Tillis, T. Graham
   Brown, Patty Loveless, and Clint Black]
1994 Album of the Year, *Common Thread: The Songs of the Eagles*
1994 Entertainer of the Year
1994 Male Vocalist of the Year
1995 Male Vocalist of the Year
1996 Song of the Year, "Go Rest High on That Mountain"
1996 Vocal Event of the Year, "I Will Always Love You"
   [Dolly Parton and Vince Gill]
1999 Vocal Event of the Year, "My Kind of Woman/My Kind of Man"
   [Patty Loveless and Vince Gill]

Grammy Awards

1990 Best Country Vocal, Male, "When I Call Your Name"
1991 Best Country Vocal Collaboration, "Restless"
   [Vince Gill, Mark O'Connor, Steve Wariner, and Ricky Skaggs]
1992 Best Country Song (Songwriter's Award), "I Still Believe in You"

1992   Best Country Vocal Performance, Male, "I Still Believe in You"

1993   Best Country Instrumental Performance, "Red Wing"
[Asleep at the Wheel and Vince Gill]

1994   Best Country Vocal Performance, Male, "When Love Finds You"

1995   Best Country Song (Songwriter's Award), "Go Rest High on That Mountain"

1995   Best Country Vocal Performance, Male, "Go Rest High on That Mountain"

1996   Best Country Vocal Performance, Male, "Worlds Apart"

1996   Best Country Collaboration with Vocals, "High Lonesome Sound" [Vince Gill, Alison Krauss & Union Station]

1997   Best Country Vocal Performance, Male, "Pretty Little Adriana"

1998   Best Country Instrumental Performance, "A Soldier's Joy"

1998   Best Country Vocal Performance, Male, "If You Ever Have Forever in Mind"

1999   Best Country Instrumental Performance, "Bob's Breakdowns" [Asleep at the Wheel and Vince Gill]

Nashville Music Awards

1994   Male Vocalist of the Year

1995   Male Vocalist of the Year

1995   Song of the Year, "Go Rest High on That Mountain"

1996   Artist/Songwriter of the Year

1996   Male Vocalist of the Year

1997   Artist/Songwriter of the Year

1997   Male Vocalist of the Year

1998   Male Vocalist of the Year

Special Honors

1993   The Harmony Award

1994   Outstanding Nashvillian of the Year, Kiwanis Club

1994   Tennessean of the Year, the Tennessee Sports Hall of Fame

1995   VH1 Honors Awards Recipient

1996   Nashville Arthritis Foundation Eighth Annual Tribute
Evening Award

1997   Oklahoma Hall of Fame

1997   Oklahoma Cowboy Hall of Fame

1997   Orville H. Gibson Lifetime Achievement Award

1997   Tennessee PGA Junior Golf Tour
Renamed: "The Vince Gill Tennessee PGA Junior Golf
Tournament"

TNN/Music City News Awards

1991   Instrumentalist of the Year

1991   Single of the Year, "When I Call Your Name"

1992   Instrumentalist of the Year

1993   Album of the Year, *I Still Believe in You*

1993   Minnie Pearl Award, For Humanitarian Efforts

1993   Single of the Year, "I Still Believe in You"

1994   Instrumentalist of the Year

1996   Best Vocal Collaboration, "Go Rest High on That Mountain"
[Patty Loveless, Vince Gill, and Ricky Skaggs]

BIBLIOGRAPHY

Books

Bego, Mark. *Country Hunks*. New York: Contemporary Books, 1994.

Biracree, Tom. *The Country Music Almanac*. Englewood Cliffs, NJ: Prentice Hall, 1993.

Byron, Janet. *The Country Music Lover's Guide to the U.S.A.* New York: St. Martin's Press, 1996.

Emery, Ralph with Patsi Bale Cox. *The View from Nashville*. New York: William Morrow, 1998 (also Los Angeles, CA: Audio Renaissance, audio tape, abridged, 1998).

Erlewine, Michael, Vladimir Bogdanov, Chris Woodstra, and Stephen Thomas Erlewine, eds. *All Music Guide to Country*. San Francisco, CA: Miller Freeman, 1997.

Kosser, Mike. *Hot Country*. New York: Avon Books, 1993.

Leamer, Laurence. *Three Chords and the Truth*. New York: HarperCollins, 1997.

Maltin, Leonard. *2000 Movie & Video Guide*. New York: Signet Books, 1999.

Rees, Dafydd, and Luke Crampton. *Encyclopedia of Rock Stars*. London, England: DK Publishing, 1996.

———. *Rock Movers & Shakers*. New York: Billboard Books, 1991.

Richards, Tad, and Melvin B. Shestack. *The New Country Music Encyclopedia*. New York: Simon & Schuster, 1993.

Sgammato, Jo. *For The Music: The Vince Gill Story*. New York: Ballantine Books, 1999.

Whitburn, Joel. *The Billboard Book of Top 40 Country Hits, 1944 to the Present.* New York: Billboard Books, 1996.

———. *Top Pop 1955–1982.* Milwaukee, WI: Record Research Inc./Banta, 1983.

———. *Top Top Albums 1955–1985.* Milwaukee, WI: Record Research, Inc./Banta, 1995.

Broadcast Sources

Late Night with David Letterman. Television talk show, CBS-TV, September 15, 1998.

"Radio Syndicated Round Table." MCA sponsored radio broadcast, May 1998.

"33rd Annual Country Music Association Awards." CBS-TV, September 22, 1999.

Internet Sources

Gill, Vince. MCA Records Press bio, off the Internet, 1998.

Grant, Amy. *Encyclopedia of Popular Music.* Internet bio. Maze UK Ltd., 1989–98.

Slawecki, Chris. "Vince Gill Announces Symphonic Christmas Tour," *Music Wire,* Internet news service, November 1996.

Vince Gill Internet page with interview, 1998. www.vincegill.com.

Interviews

Bennett, Pete. New York City, August 1998.

Frank, Suzy, telephone. August 25, 1998.

Gill, Vince. Tucson, AZ, January 1995.

Liner Notes And Press Bios

Benson, Ray. *Tribute to Bob Wills,* by Asleep at the Wheel, Liberty
    Records, 1993.
Cash, Rosanne, and Rodney Crowell. *Turn Me Loose,* by Vince Gill.
    Album liner notes, RCA Records, 1984.
Escott, Colin. *The Essential Vince Gill.* CD liner notes,
    RCA Records, 1995.
Gill, Vince. *Let There Be Peace on Earth,* by Vince Gill. Liner notes,
    MCA Records, 1993.
————. MCA Records press bio, July 1998.
Streisand, Barbra. *A Love Like Ours,* by Barbra Streisand. Liner notes,
    Columbia Records, 1999.

Periodicals

Allen, Bob. "Vince Gill: One of the Boys." *Country Music,*
    March/April 1997.
Allman, Kevin. "Backstage with a Rising Country Rock Star."
    Los Angeles Times, September 20, 1993.
Barnes, Deborah. "Vince Charming—Is He Nashville's Next
    Mayor/Citizen Vince." *New Country,* June 1997.
Barnes, Deborah and Tamara Saviano. "Vince Gill: I'm Just Having Fun."
    Country Weekly, December 1, 1998.
Blosser, John, and Bennet Bolton. "Country Star Vince Gill, Heartbreak
    to . . . the Top." *National Enquirer,* December 28, 1993.
Buk, Askokd. "Vince Gill: Influential, Incredible, InVINCEible!"
    Country Guitar, Summer 1995.
Chicago Tribune. Chicago, IL, September 13, 1990.
Cochran, Beth E. "Vince Gill: Going the Distance." *Upbeat,*
    January 1998.
"Country Notes: Water's No Hazard to Golf-Loving Vince."
    Country Weekly, September 22, 1998.
Cromelin, Richard. "Dedicated to Just Plain Folks." Calendar Section:
    Los Angeles Times, September 24, 1994.

Flans, Robyn. "The Very Entertaining Vince Gill." *Country Fever*, May/June 1994.

———. "Surprise . . . Dolly's Turning 50 . . . And Still Country's Most Gorgeous Whirlwind / Dolly: Gorgeous Dynamo Nears 50." *Country Weekly*, August 29, 1995.

Flippo, Chet. "Gill on More Traditional Path." *Los Angeles Daily News*, July 9, 1998.

Greenblatt, Mike. "Handsome Superstar Vince Gill." *Modern Screen's Country*, May 1992.

———. "Loving Father Vince Gill Admits . . . the Price He Pays to Be a Star." *Modern Screen's Country*, Fall 1991.

———. "Vince Gill Gets into the Christmas Spirit." *Modern Screen's Country*, March 1994.

———. "Vince Gill Wins One 'for the Pickers'." *Modern Screen's Country*, March 1992.

Gregor, Pat. "Olivia to Vince: You're the One That I Want!—Sources Say." *Globe*, June 21, 1998.

Haislop, Neil. "Vince Gill." *Country Fever*, February 1993.

Hillburn, Robert. "Checking in with . . . Vince Gill: Songs in the Key of Life." *Los Angeles Times*, August 2, 1998.

Hitts, Roger. "Ashley Judd in Hot New Romance with Amy Grant's Ex." *Star*, April 20, 1999.

———. "I Fled in Terror from Raging Vince Gill." *Star*, June 22, 1999.

———. "Vince Gill Walks Out on Wife for Rock Beauty." *Star*, May 6, 1997.

Holden, Larry. "Vince Gill the Modest Achiever—15 Years of Gold and Platinum." *Country Weekly*, February 9, 1999.

Holden, Larry, and Bob Campbell. "Golfin' Vince Gill and Friends Score Big for Charity." *Country Weekly*, August 31, 1999.

Kaplan, Michael. "Vince Gill: Sweetheart of the Country Music Awards." *TV Guide*, September 25, 1993.

———. "Vince Gill: The Nicest Guy in Nashville." *TV Guide*, October 1, 1994.

"Kraft Country Tour '97 Presents Vince Gill," [a special advertising section by tour sponsor, Kraft Foods]. *New Country*, July 1997.

Lanham, Tom, "One More Last Chance/The Reinvention of Vince Gill." *New Country,* 1996.

Lexington Herald-Leader. Lexington, KY, July 19, 1990).

"Magical Sleigh Tracks, Fake Snow, and Sickly Trees." *Country Weekly,* December 22, 1996.

Mansfield, Brian. "Country Pumps Up the Sales Volume." *USA Today,* December 29, 1998.

Morden, Darryl. "Vince Gill." Concert review, *Hollywood Reporter,* July 13, 1998.

———. "Vince Gill." Concert review, *Hollywood Reporter,* July 12, 1999.

Morris, Edward. "Vince's Pomp & Country Stance." *Country Weekly,* July 27, 1999.

Morse, Steve. "Time For a Change." *LA Life/Daily News* [reprinting a story from the *Boston Globe*], August 4, 1996.

Newcomer, Wendy. "Restless Heart Back on the Road with No End." *Country Weekly,* August 4, 1998.

Ray, Daniel P. and Tamara Saviano. "Vince Gill Unlocks a Traditional Country Sound with *The Key.*" *Country Weekly,* August 18, 1998.

Rodak, Jeffrey. "Wife's Nasty Anniversary Gift to Vince Gill: A Divorce!" *National Enquirer,* May 6, 1997.

Russell, Deborah. "A&M, Myrrh Build Amy Grant's *House of Love* on Solid Ground." *Billboard,* July 30, 1994.

Sanz, Cynthia and Jane Sanderson. "Vince and Janis Gill." *People,* June 10, 1991.

Saviano, Tamara. "Amy Kurland: Lady Sings The Blues." *Playgirl,* August 1998.

———. "CMA Awards 'Entertainer Of The Year'—Profile of the Contenders (Vince Gill)." *Country Weekly,* September 22, 1998.

———. "It's Going to Be a Blast for Vince Gill/A Clean Shirt and New Music . . . Vince Gill's Back on the Road." *Country Weekly,* June 2, 1998.

Saviano, Tamara, and Deborah Barnes. "The Vinny's Another Birdie That Gill Scores for Charity." *Country Weekly,* September 1, 1998.

Sievert, Jon. "Vince Gill, Picking the Hits." *The Best of Guitar Player,* "Country" issue, 1993.

Smith, Lisa. "Vince Gill." *Gavin Report,* March 8, 1991.

"Turn Out the Lights: After 17 Years of Marriage, Singers Vince Gill and Wife Janis Go Down Separate Country Roads." *People,* May 5, 1997.

Varga, George. "Vince Gill Gets Serious." *San Diego Union Tribune,* 1996.

"Vin (Not So) Ordinaire." People Country [special issue of *People*], Fall 1994.

"Vince Gill: CMA Awards Entertainer of the Year." *Country Weekly,* 1996.

"Vince Gill Cuts Back on Work to Save Marriage to His Sweetheart of the Rodeo." *Star,* March 30, 1993.

"Vince Gill: New Album Helps Me over Brother's Death." *Star,* November 16, 1993.

"Vince Gill's Heart-Stopping Search for Mom After Blast." *Star,* May 16, 1995.

Wood, Gerry. "Vince Gill in His Own Words/The World According to Vince." *Country Weekly,* August 17, 1999.

———. "Vince Gill: The New Me/Vince Gill's Big Adventure." *Country Weekly,* June 25, 1996.

Wood, Gerry, and Wendy Newcomer. "Vince Gill's Rarin' to Go/Vince Gill Gears Up to Take the Country by Storm Again." *Country Weekly,* March 3, 1998.

Zimmerman, David. "Gill and Yearwood, Poised for a Big Year." *USA Today,* September 1, 1992.

INDEX

ABOUT THE AUTHOR

Mark Bego is the author of several bestselling books on rock 'n' roll and show business. With thirty-eight books published and more than ten million copies in print, he is the bestselling biographer in the rock and pop music field. His first Top Ten *New York Times* bestseller was *Michael!* about Michael Jackson (1984). Since then he has written *Cher!* (1986), *Rock Hudson: Public & Private* (1986), *Bette Midler: Outrageously Divine* (1987), *Aretha Franklin: Queen of Soul* (1989), *Madonna: Blonde Ambition* (1992), and *Jewel* (1998).

In the 1990s Bego branched out into country-music books, writing *Country Hunks* (1994), *Country Gals* (1995), *I Fall to Pieces: The Music and the Life of Patsy Cline* (1995), *Alan Jackson: Gone Country* (1996), *George Strait: The Story of Country's Living Legend* (1997), and *LeAnn Rimes* (1998).

Mark has co-authored books with several rock stars including Martha Reeves *(Martha Reeves: Dancing in the Street: Confessions of a Motown Diva),* Micky Dolenz of the Monkees (*I'm a Believer,* 1993), Jimmy Greenspoon of Three Dog Night (*One Is the Loneliest Number,* 1991), and Mary Wilson (*Dreamgirl: My Life As a Supreme,* 1999 edition).

In 1998, Bego wrote *Leonardo DiCaprio: Romantic Hero,* which spent six weeks on the *New York Times* bestseller list. He followed it up with *Matt Damon: Chasing a Dream* and *Will Smith: The Freshest Prince.* His most recent book is *Cher: If You Believe.* Also in 1998, Melitta Coffee launched Mark Bego: Romantic Hero blend coffee as part of their Celebrity Series.

Mark Bego divides his time between New York City, Los Angeles, and Tucson, Arizona. Visit his Web site at: www/internethoster.com/Bego/.